P•O•E•T•R•Y
for GUYS

P•O•E•T•R•Y
for GUYS

...who thought they hated poetry

Compiled and with commentary by

Kathleen Grizzard Schmook

WILLOW CREEK PRESS

MINOCQUA, WISCONSIN

© 1996 Willow Creek Press

Kim Leighton, Editor

Published in 1996 by Willow Creek Press
P.O. Box 147, Minocqua, Wisconsin 54548

For information on other Willow Creek titles,
call 1-800-850-WILD

ISBN 1-57223-065-7

Library of Congress Cataloging-in-Publication Data

Poetry for guys -- who thought they hated poetry / compiled and
    with commentary by Kathleen Grizzard Schmook.
        p.   cm.
    1. Men—Poetry.   2. Masculinity (Psychology)—Poetry.
    3. American poetry—Men authors.   4. English poetry—Men
    authors.   I. Schmook, Kathy Grizzard.
    PS590.P64   1996
    811.008'09286--dc20   96-42279
                                                        CIP

Printed in the U.S.A.

Contents

><+>-O-<+><

Introduction

Poetry For Guys is just that, a meticulous compilation of important verse penned over the years that provides a high-octane kick in the soul. Some of the selections do so with a bang, others with a whisper. But breathe easy, guys: We practice safe verse.

So go ahead, flip through the chapters. This book won't bite. And if you want to, carry it around the bookstore for awhile and get used to cradling a collection of poetry. Don't look sheepish. No one will throw anything at you.

But after reading a few selections, you will want to kick back and give these poems more than a quick read. In fact, you'll find this work will become an important part of your library. And how nice to hold something that doesn't age, isn't trendy, and won't give you a headache in the morning. This unassuming little book seeks only to renew your spirit while reacquainting you with life's simpler pleasures.

Don't be intimidated. There's something here for everyone, from stevedores to Sybarites. You'll enjoy these poems even if you never took an English Lit class, even if you never went to school.

Why, you'll enjoy them even if you have no teeth, though you might want to borrow some to chew your wife out for not buying you a book of poetry before.

She may be harboring the idea that you are a worthless couch potato. Make the transition and become a bed spud. Languish in your dressing gown and sip a single-malt Scotch while enjoying Robert Frost, Carl Sandburg, or Edgar Allan Poe. Or lounge around in those boxer shorts with the droopy elastic, nurse a home brew and a cheap cigar along with the galvanic style of Robert Service, the unique verse of Richard Brautigan, and the inimitable satire of Greg Keeler.

Look on this as a self-help book. If you think you're emotionally deficient, heal thyself through its pages and throw off the shackles of your phone-sex cord.

I mean, you think you've got it bad? Some of these poets add new dimensions to the states of despair, disquiet, and desertion. But rather than bemoan their vicissitudes, they paint their sentiments on the canvas of our hearts with magnificent words and phrases.

Now, you ask, where does a female fit in?

Well, I'm like a literary condom, your protection against any hidden male narcissism. The editor told me that my job in *Poetry for Guys* is to "explain you to you" from a woman's perspective. So I'll be your escort through this book. And if I've done my job, I'll make you think, make you mad, make you laugh and, most important, make you feel.

Just think of me as the muse with the news, boys.

Actually, a sincere love of poetry has taught me to appreciate the intricacies of rhyme and particularly rhythm, which I have practiced for many years. And I am confident that commentary throughout *Poetry For Guys* will convince you that onomatopoeia does not require Blue Star ointment, and that a couplet is not a training bra.

And trust me. The women in your life will be impressed by your purchase of this book. We are totally turned on by men who tune into more than ESPN. My guess is that after reading this book you'll never look at snowy woods, foggy harbors, or heaving orbs in the same way (well, maybe the latter is the exception). Perhaps it will rekindle memories of lost loves or reignite the hope of discovering new ones.

Turn the page now and join me on a journey through centuries of adventure, valor, and romance. And though it may appear to be down a road less travelled, aren't those always the most memorable?

—Kathy Grizzard Schmook

ARS POETICA

A poem should be palpable and mute
As a globed fruit,

Dumb
As old medallions to the thumb,

Silent as the sleeve-worn stone
Of casement ledges where the moss has grown—

A poem should be wordless
As the flight of birds.

A poem should be motionless in time
As the moon climbs,

Leaving, as the moon releases
Twig by twig the night-entangled trees,

Leaving, as the moon behind the winter leaves,
Memory by memory the mind—

A poem should be motionless in time
As the moon climbs.

A poem should be equal to:
Not true.

For all the history of grief
An empty doorway and a maple leaf.

For love
The leaning grasses and two lights above the sea—

A poem should not mean
But be.

— Archibald MacLeish

"How They Play"

➤–◆➤–O–◆➤–◄

N o, of course I don't believe that men only think about sports and sex. Money figures in there somewhere. But regardless of their level of interest, ardent jock or weekend dilettante, their sports are serious business, an almost spiritual obsession, obliging some to enshrine them in verse.

Unlike women, who must carefully orchestrate free time, men operate without the need for such orderliness. They'll eat beenie-weenies for a week if it affords them a new rifle, a set of clubs, or a new fishing rod.

They will budget for that snappy little bass boat. Heaven for them is a day on the lake, barefoot, in a T-shirt and Bermuda shorts, fueled by beer and pork rinds. When purchasing red wigglers or any other live bait, red, rubber flip-flops seem to be de rigueur.

And pardon me, but hasn't this FLY-fishing thing gotten a bit out of hand? These guys truly believe that the hours spent fishing will never be subtracted from their allotted time. And to think it was sex in the '60s!

Even our contemporary poets pay homage to a scaly, slimy

creature with a steely glare and malocclusion. And they wax poetic over the bait, for God's sake, making an art form of things killed with a fly swatter. They give them names usually associated with the contents of a handkerchief. Hell, they spend half their lives catching these fish, then they let 'em go. Go figure.

Give a man a cigar, even a cheesy one, and life becomes leisure. Put him on a Harley, and his testosterone level soars. Give him a rod or a gun, and he moves to Montana. Add some camo and a bullet bandolier, and he becomes an anarchist staring down the barrel of a CNN camera.

And there are the former athletes who wistfully recall their chance at pro ball. I always wonder if they really gave it up due to an injury or if they just had the coordination of a fainting goat.

Regardless, once-upon-a-time jocks eventually settle into the game of golf, which seems odd for someone with an allegedly bad passing arm. But man, do they get into it. One avid golfing friend avowed that it was "the most fun a guy can have standing up." Hmmm. I and other women might argue.

So enjoy the poetry of pastimes, from Davies' yuppie lament "Leisure," (penned, strangely enough, decades before there were such creatures) to Keeler's musings, which may urge you to spawn.

—-kgs

LEISURE

What is this life if, full of care,
We have no time to stand and stare.

No time to stand beneath the boughs
And stare as long as sheep or cows.

No time to see, when woods we pass,
Where squirrels hide their nuts in grass.

No time to see, in broad daylight,
Streams full of stars like skies at night.

No time to turn at Beauty's glance,
And watch her feet, how they can dance.

No time to wait till her mouth can
Enrich that smile her eyes began.

A poor life this if, full of care,
We have no time to stand and stare.

— William Henry Davies

LA-Z-BOY

Let mine be as
automatic as possible,
and lay me not down
till I'm dying.
Then perhaps you may
rock me a little
so that I'll know
(momentarily)
what it is to be steady.
Let my last worldly
possessions
be a beer on my right
popcorn on my left
to sustain me
when I kick back
for that long last
Late Show.
And let me decay thus:
not sitting,
not standing,
not Lying,
but somewhere between—
reclining—
like an astronaut
in a reverse lift-off,
in the posture of
convenience,
a dyed-in-the-wool
dead-in-the-velour
La-Z-Boy.

— Greg Keeler

CONFESSION OF THE BORN-AGAIN PURIST

Forgive me for I have been
in the company of worms
and have carried them in a can
and have touched them
with my fingers
and have made them to
part in small pieces
and have pierced those pieces
with the barbs of hooks.
And I have had impure thoughts
about the body of a fish
and have desired to make it
part of my body.
Thus I made a pierced piece
of worm to dangle before it
so that it ate thereof,
and I made it to
come unto my hand,
and I smote it
with a large stick
to make it still,
and I slit it with my knife,
and I plucked the entrails
from its belly,
and I made my thumb
to run up its spine,
and I rinsed it
that it might be free of blood,
and I made it to roll
in cornmeal and flour,
and I let it fall in hot grease,
and I held it unto my lips,
and I ate thereof.

— Greg Keeler

FOR THE CRAWLERS

We've watered the lawn for you again.
And even in the sun you're wallowing
up and rooting the grass for rot.
It's your luck the robins don't
like us or the yard would turn
Italian dinner. We've seen
you sliding over the cool, wet
evenings of America,
crazed children with flashlights
homing in. Some day their youth,
touched, will shoot back like you do.
Our shrinks choose snakes, the fools.
They are insomniacs but never take
the time to go out and look down
into the grass at midnight.
Sometimes you appear as fishnets,
bellied out over our gardens
toward the moon. And after rain
your deaths are as worthless as
broken shoelaces on our sidewalks.
To bring you up, we've played the earth
like a fiddle on boards and buried
electrodes in our back yards.
We've dozened you up in styrofoam cups.
We've even made quiche out of you.
You poor sonofabitches.
For you, crucifixion would be peanuts.
We've pinched you apart,
slipped your gobs on hooks
and spit on you for good luck.

— Greg Keeler

FOR ABRAHAM AND IZAAK WALTON

And lo he took his sons unto the brook
and bade them fish quietly and patiently.
And when their lines many times
had encircled the ends of their poles
and their reels had made many tangles,
he wept before them saying, "That son
who unto me would bring peace, he shall
I call unto the station wagon
and give candy and pop."
And lo a wond'rous silence fell
upon them, for they knew not why
their father would spread his bounty
before them for not fishing.
And then it was that many heavy fish
came unto his bait and many sounds came
unto him from the station wagon.
And the sounds of empty candy
wrappers begat many pitches both high
and low of grumbling.
And the grumbling begat lamentations of
the late hour, and the late hour begat a
longing for that which they had come to call TV.
And lo he walked unto the car and
spake unto them saying many words
of which he had not thought himself capable.
And in his anger, he threw his rod
unto the back and made the door
to slam upon it.

— Greg Keeler

"What Am I?"

Poems about nature are a balm for our tattered souls. Soothing and subtle, they trace images of the ethereal and breathe new dimensions into rainbows, flowers, wind, rain, and trees. Simple pleasures, are they not?

So how come you guys have lost your way?

Now let's not blame today's ill-defined male role on women's liberation. I've given three guys their freedom myself. Just admit it — you got tired of opening car doors and pulling out chairs. You long to return to your roots, your caveman/provider thing, dragging us around by the hair.

Perhaps some of you are involved with the "Men's Movement," which I always thought meant a successful trip to the lavatory. But I've come to understand that it is more an attempt to bond with your inner selves, a primal thing.

Well fine, boys. Get thee to a tom-tom and let the beat go on. Stand in the woods, hold hands if you must, and stare at a carved phallic symbol and accept the fact that all men are not created equal, then get over it. Hell, Hiawatha did! *Poetry For Guys* is here to help you stop and smell the roses without getting thorns in your noses.

So, for now, rein in your prurient interests and realize that getting in touch with Mother Nature is not a matter of ogling the Sports Illustrated swimsuit edition.

Most of the poetry in this chapter celebrates the unsullied natural world of yesteryear and proves that beauty is where we find it. Other selections are more contemporary, such as Keeler's "For The Armadillos," a critter known in some parts as possum on the half-shell.

Relax now, and leave the confines of your asphalt jungle. Return to an earlier time when you were awed by simpler things. And yes, if a loincloth beckons, tie one on.

And if you get carried away and feel compelled to mark your territory, go outside — after dark.

—kgs

THE TIGER

Tiger, Tiger, burning bright
In the forests of the night;
What immortal hand or eye,
Could frame thy fearful symmetry?

In what distant deeps or skies
Burnt the fire of thine eyes?
On what wings dare he aspire?
What the hand, dare seize the fire?

And what shoulder, & what art,
Could twist the sinews of thy heart?
And when thy heart began to beat,
What dread hand? & what dread feet?

What the hammer? what the chain?
In what furnace was thy brain?
What the anvil? what dread grasp
Dare its deadly terrors clasp?

When the stars threw down their spears
And water'd heaven with their tears:
Did he smile his work to see?
Did he who made the Lamb make thee?

Tiger, Tiger, burning bright,
In the forests of the night:
What immortal hand or eye,
Dare frame thy fearful symmetry?

— William Blake

I STROVE WITH NONE

I strove with none, for none was worth my strife:
    Nature I loved, and next to Nature, Art:
I warmed both hands before the fire of Life;
    It sinks; and I am ready to depart.

— Walter Savage Landor

YES, THE FISH MUSIC

A trout-colored wind blows
through my eyes, through my fingers,
and I remember how the trout
used to hide from the dinosaurs
when they came to drink at the river.
The trout hid in subways, castles
and automobiles. They waited patiently
for the dinosaurs to go away.

— Richard Brautigan

THE BULL

It is in captivity—
ringed, haltered, chained
to a drag
the bull is godlike

Unlike the cows
he lives alone, nozzles
the sweet grass gingerly
to pass the time away

He kneels, lies down
and stretching out
a foreleg licks himself
about the hoof

then stays
with half-closed eyes,
Olympian commentary on
the bright passage of days.

—The round sun
smooths his lacquer
through
the glossy pinetrees

his substance hard
as ivory or glass—
through which the wind
yet plays—
        Milkless

he nods
the hair between his horns
and eyes matted
with hyacinthine curls

— William Carlos Williams

DO NOT ASK

Do not ask for whom they moo
or why they stand and chew and chew.
They've got their plans; their heads are clear.
Their future moves from mouth to rear.
Somewhat like ours (like ours I mean
who see no more than what we've seen,
who do our best till noon then run
to eat that beef between those buns
then do our best into the night
before the T.V.'s tiny light).
They munch the purple clover in
then splatter it right out again,
not quite as pretty as it was,
at most a place for flies to buzz.
But God, they're stable on four feet,
no philosophical elite
to make them wonder why they chew
and urinate the way they do
or sit and ponder what they're worth.
No, cows just occupy the earth:
the same earth, by the way, which one
fine day will melt into the sun.

— Greg Keeler

STOPPING BY WOODS ON A SNOWY EVENING

Whose woods these are I think I know.
His house is in the village, though;
He will not see me stopping here
To watch his woods fill up with snow.

My little horse must think it queer
To stop without a farmhouse near
Between the woods and frozen lake
The darkest evening of the year.

He gives his harness bells a shake
To ask if there is some mistake.
The only other sound's the sweep
Of easy wind and downy flake.

The woods are lovely, dark and deep,
But I have promises to keep,
And miles to go before I sleep,
And miles to go before I sleep.

—Robert Frost

FOR THE ARMADILLOS

We've noticed how
you've come up as far as Kansas
curled in maimed half-moons by the road.
What do you do that for?
Won't the bobcat still peel you
slick as abalone?
Won't you still surprise us
like a walking rock
or shock us as you bolt from ditches,
running like we never knew you could?
Go ahead and butt your snout into
those bugs for now.
Go ahead and make your little
feet rattle through burrs and thistles
while your body floats like
the moon above them.
But what did you come here for?
To have some farm girl fling
you wounded from a bridge
on the Cimarron,
thinking that she is doing
you a favor,
thinking that you
are some kind of half-assed
nightmare turtle?
Some folks say you taste like rabbit.
Others say you carry leprosy,
but most of us just glimpse
a bubble and ears poking up
from the asphalt
and drive on.

— Greg Keeler

THE EAGLE

He clasps the crag with crooked hands;
Close to the sun in lonely lands,
Ringed with the azure world, he stands.

The wrinkled sea beneath him crawls;
He watches from his mountain walls,
And like a thunderbolt he falls.

— Lord Alfred Tennyson

THE QUAIL

There are three quail in a cage next door,
and they are the sweet delight of our mornings,
calling to us like small frosted cakes:
bobwhitebobwhitebobwhite,
but at night they drive our Got-damn cat Jake crazy.
They run around that cage like pinballs
as he stands out there,
smelling their asses through the wire.

— Richard Brautigan

MY HEART LEAPS UP

My heart leaps up when I behold
    A rainbow in the sky:
So was it when my life began;
So is it now I am a man;
So be it when I shall grow old.
    Or let me die!
The Child is father of the Man;
And I could wish my days to be
Bound each to each by natural piety.

— William Wordsworth

FOG

The fog comes
on little cat feet.

It sits looking
over harbor and city
on silent haunches
and then moves on.

— Carl Sandburg

THE NATURE POEM

The moon
is Hamlet
on a motorcycle
coming down
a dark road.
He is wearing
a black leather
jacket and
boots.
I have
nowhere
to go.
I will ride
all night.

— Richard Brautigan

THE SONG OF HIAWATHA
INTRODUCTION

Should you ask me, whence these stories?
Whence these legends and traditions,
With the odors of the forest,
With the dew and damp of meadows,
With the curling smoke of wigwams,
With the rushing of great rivers,
With their frequent repetitions,
And their wild reverberations,
As of thunder in the mountains?

I should answer, I should tell you,
"From the forests and the prairies,
From the great lakes of the Northland,
From the land of the Ojibways,
From the land of the Dacotahs,
From the mountains, moors, and fen-lands
Where the heron, the Shuh-shuh-gah,
Feeds among the reeds and rushes.
I repeat them as I heard them
From the lips of Nawadaha,
The musician, the sweet singer."

Should you ask where Nawadaha
Found these songs so wild and wayward,
Found these legends and traditions,
I should answer, I should tell you,
"In the bird's-nests of the forest,
In the lodges of the beaver,
In the hoof-prints of the bison,
In the eyry of the eagle!

"All the wild-fowl sang them to him,
In the moorlands and the fen-lands,
In the melancholy marshes;
Chetowaik, the plover, sang them,
Mahng, the loon, the wild-goose, Wawa,
The blue heron, the Shuh-shuh-gah,
And the grouse, the Mushkodasa!"

If still further you should ask me,
Saying, "Who was Nawadaha?
Tell us of this Nawadaha,"
I should answer your inquiries
Straightway in such words as follow.

"In the Vale of Tawasentha,
In the green and silent valley,
By the pleasant water-courses,
Dwelt the singer Nawadaha.
Round about the Indian village
Spread the meadows and the corn-fields,
And beyond them stood the forest,
Stood the groves of singing pine-trees,
Green in Summer, white in Winter,
Ever sighing, ever singing.

"And the pleasant water-courses,
You could trace them through the valley,
By the rushing in the Spring-time,
By the alders in the Summer,
By the white fog in the Autumn,
By the black line in the Winter;
And beside them dwelt the singer,
In the Vale of Tawasentha,
In the green and silent valley.

"There he sang of Hiawatha,
Sang the Song of Hiawatha,
Sang his wondrous birth and being,
How he prayed and how he fasted,
How he lived, and toiled, and suffered,
That the tribes of men might prosper,
That he might advance his people!"

Ye who love the haunts of Nature,
Love the sunshine of the meadow,
Love the shadow of the forest,
Love the wind among the branches,
And the rain-shower and the snow-storm,
And the rushing of great rivers
Through their palisades of pine-trees,
And the thunder in the mountains,
Whose innumerable echoes
Flap like eagles in their eyries;—
Listen to these wild traditions,
To this Song of Hiawatha!

Ye who love a nation's legends,
Love the ballads of a people,
That like voices from afar off
Call to us to pause and listen,
Speak in tones so plain and childlike,
Scarcely can the ear distinguish
Whether they are sung or spoken;—
Listen to this Indian Legend,
To this Song of Hiawatha!

Ye whose hearts are fresh and simple,
Who have faith in God and Nature,
Who believe, that in all ages
Every human heart is human,
That in even savage bosoms
There are longings, yearnings, strivings
For the good they comprehend not,
That the feeble hands and helpless,
Groping blindly in the darkness,
Touch God's right hand in that darkness
And are lifted up and strengthened;—
Listen to this simple story,
To this Song of Hiawatha!

Ye, who sometimes, in your rambles
Through the green lanes of the country,
Where the tangled barberry-bushes
Hang their tufts of crimson berries
Over stone walls gray with mosses,
Pause by some neglected graveyard,
For a while to muse, and ponder
On a half-e~aced inscription,
Written with little skill of song-craft,
Homely phrases, but each letter
Full of hope and yet of heart-break,
Full of all the tender pathos
Of the Here and the Hereafter;—
Stay and read this rude inscription,
Read this Song of Hiawatha!

—Henry Wadsworth Longfellow

"What They Salute"

><del>◄►◄del>►◄del>○◄del>◄◄►◄del>◄

I t appears that American patriotism is on wobbly legs, so thank goodness there's poetry as the great equalizer, a form of expression that plays ring-around-the-rhetoric with what some might call heresy.

As a nation founded by revolutionary dissidents, our course will likely never be smooth. But we endure due to a sense of fair play as Americans and by hewing to the concepts of the Constitution of the United States, even though we're unaware of it most of the time.

Besides, as a young country, where is our sense of humility? In the big scheme of things, we're barely potty trained. We're the polyester of Western civilization.

And our domestic issues are so lame we can fight those battles on television talk shows. Actually, we argue over things that a spanking would solve.

Well, that's OK, it's part of our nature to poke fun at the good old U.S.A. But those snooty Brits and Europeans can't! The French are still sour grapes over the real-men-don't-eat-quiche issue, and the English — who insist on referring to us as the "colonies" - are still pissed off that we won the war, for God's sake!

But the real threat is not another country; it's "political correctness." By PC standards, the Pledge of Allegiance has been deemed a civil rights infringement that many would like to see replaced by a daily reading of the Miranda Rights in school rooms.

Besides PC, there is our deification of stars. Where are we going with this?

Even our postage stamp has lost its sense of history. Images of the flag and our forefathers have been replaced with the likes of Elvis, who deified a hound dog in song and literally fell off his throne. And there's Marilyn, who popped out of a birthday cake for a president, later rumored to have a guppy-like libido. Both Elvis and Marilyn met untimely deaths due to substance abuse, which has, sadly, become as American as apple pie.

Our greatest patriots nowadays may be the people here who don't speak English. After spending weeks on a raft in the ocean for the privilege of mowing someone's grass, painting their house, and living in an abandoned bus, these folks get the big picture and appreciate what we Americans are complacent about.

Occasionally, my faith in patriotism is revived at sporting events, particularly baseball games, when men remove their caps and place their hand over their hearts during the national anthem, which is now sung by people who think George Washington Carver was a U.S. president who made duck decoys as a hobby.

But the poetry that follows reacquaints us with our nation's birth and memorable figures like Ralph Waldo Emerson, whose moving first stanza in "Concord Hymn," referring to the shot heard 'round the world, causes me to wonder if there will be another sound so powerful in our future. At the rate we're going, we can look forward to Lisa Marie Presley being shot from a cannon during halftime at the Super Bowl.

Enjoy the following collection, a sonogram that records our country's heartbeat.

—kgs

O CAPTAIN! MY CAPTAIN!

O Captain! my Captain! our fearful trip is done,
The ship has weather'd every rack, the prize we sought is won,
The port is near, the bells I hear, the people all exulting,
While follow eyes the steady keel, the vessel grim and daring;
    But O heart! heart! heart!
        O the bleeding drops of red,
            Where on the deck my Captain lies,
                Fallen cold and dead.

O Captain! my Captain! rise up and hear the bells;
Rise up—for you the flag is flung—for you the bugle trills,
For you bouquets and ribbon'd wreaths—for you the shores
a-crowding,
For you they call, the swaying mass, their eager faces turning;
    Here Captain! dear father!
        This arm beneath your head!
            It is some dream that on the deck,
                You've fallen cold and dead.

My Captain does not answer, his lips are pale and still,
My father does not feel my arm, he has no pulse nor will,
The ship is anchor'd safe and sound, its voyage closed and
    done,
From fearful trip the victor ship comes in with object won;
    Exult O shores, and ring O bells!
        But I with mournful tread,
            Walk the deck my Captain lies,
                Fallen cold and dead.

— Walt Whitman

CHICAGO

Hog Butcher for the World,
Tool Maker, Stacker of Wheat,
Player with Railroads and the Nation's Freight Handler;
Stormy, husky, brawling,
City of the Big Shoulders:

They tell me you are wicked and I believe them, for I have seen
your painted women under the gas lamps luring the farm
boys.

And they tell me you are crooked and I answer: Yes, it is true I
have seen the gunman kill and go free to kill again.

And they tell me you are brutal and my reply is: On the faces of
women and children I have seen the marks of wanton
hunger.

And having answered so I turn once more to those who sneer at
this my ciy, and I give them back the sneer and say to them:

Come and show me another ciy with lifted head singing so
proud to be alive and coarse and strong and cunning.

Flinging magnetic curses amid the toil of piling job on job, here
is a tall bold slugger set vivid against the little soft cities;

Fierce as a dog with tongue lapping for action, cunning as a
    savage pitted against the wilderness,
        Bareheaded,
        Shoveling,
        Wrecking,
        Planning,
        Building, breaking, rebuilding,

Under the smoke, dust all over his mouth, laughing with white
    teeth,
Under the terrible burden of destiny laughing as a young man
    laughs,
Laughing even as an ignorant fighter laughs who has never lost
    a battle,
Bragging and laughing that under his wrist is the pulse, and
under his ribs the heart of the people,
        Laughing!
Laughing the stormy, husky, brawling laughter of Youth, half
    naked, sweating, proud to be Hog Butcher, Tool Maker,
    Stacker of Wheat, Player with Railroads and Freight
    Handler to the Nation.

                — Carl Sandburg

PAUL REVERE'S RIDE

Listen, my children, and you shall hear
Of the midnight ride of Paul Revere,
On the eighteenth of April, in Seventy-five;
Hardly a man is now alive
Who remembers that famous day and year.

He said to his friend, "If the British march
By land or sea from the town tonight,
Hang a lantern aloft in the belfry arch
Of the North Church tower as a signal light,—
One, if by land, and two, if by sea;
And I on the opposite shore will be,
Ready to ride and spread the alarm
Through every Middlesex village and farm,
For the country folk to be up and to arm."

Then he said, "Good night!" and with muffled oar
Silently rowed to the Charlestown shore,
Just as the moon rose over the bay,
Where swinging wide at her moorings lay
The Somerset, British man-of-war;
A phantom ship, with each mast and spar
Across the moon like a prison bar,
And a huge black hulk, that was magnified
By its own reflection in the tide.

Meanwhile, his friend through alley and street
Wanders and watches, with eager ears,
Till in the silence around him he hears
The muster of men at the barrack door,
The sound of arms, and the tramp of feet,

And the measured tread of the grenadiers,
Marching down to their boats on the shore.

Then he climbed the tower of the Old North Church,
By the wooden stairs, with stealthy tread,
To the belfry-chamber overhead,
And startled the pigeons from their perch
On the sombre rafters, that round him made
Masses and moving shapes of shade,—
By the trembling ladder, steep and tall,
To the highest window in the wall,
Where he paused to listen and look down
A moment on the roofs of the town
And the moonlight flowing over all.

Beneath, in the churchyard, lay the dead,
In their night-encampment on the hill,
Wrapped in silence so deep and still
That he could hear, like a sentinel's tread,
The watchful night-wind, as it went
Creeping along from tent to tent,
And seeming to whisper, "All is well!"
A moment only he feels the spell
Of the place and the hour, and the secret dread
Of the lonely belfry and the dead;
For suddenly all his thoughts are bent
On a shadowy something far away,
Where the river widens to meet the bay,—
A line of black that bends and floats
On the rising tide, like a bridge of boats.

Meanwhile, impatient to mount and ride,
Booted and spurred, with a heavy stride

On the opposite shore walked Paul Revere.
Now he patted his horse's side,
Now gazed at the landscape far and near,
Then, impetuous, stamped the earth,
And turned and tightened his saddle girth;
But mostly he watched with eager search
The belfry's tower of the Old North Church,
As it rose above the graves on the hill,
Lonely and spectral and sombre and still.
And lo! as he looks, on the belfry height
A glimmer, and then a gleam of light!
He springs to the saddle, the bridle he turns,
But lingers and gazes, till full on his sight
A second lamp in the belfry burns!

A hurry of hoofs in a village street,
A shape in the moonlight, a bulk in the dark,
And beneath, from the pebbles, in passing, a spark
Struck out by a steed flying fearless and fleet;
That was all! And yet, through the gloom and the light,
The fate of a nation was riding that night;
And the spark struck out by that steed, in his flight,
Kindled the land into flame with its heat.
He has left the village and mounted the steep,
And beneath him, tranquil and broad and deep,
Is the Mystic, meeting the ocean tides;
And under the alders that skirt its edge,
Now soft on the sand, now loud on the ledge,
Is heard the tramp of his steed as he rides.

It was twelve by the village clock,
When he crossed the bridge into Medford town.
He heard the crowing of the cock,

And the barking of the farmer's dog,
And he felt the damp of the river fog,
That rises after the sun goes down.

It was one by the village clock,
When he galloped into Lexington.
He saw the gilded weathercock
Swim in the moonlight as he passed,
And the meeting-house windows, blank and bare,
Gaze at him with a spectral glare,
As if they already stood aghast
At the bloody work they would look upon.

It was two by the village clock,
When he came to the bridge in Concord town.
He heard the bleating of the flock,
And the twitter of birds among the trees,
And felt the breath of the morning breeze
Blowing over the meadows brown.
And one was safe and asleep in his bed
Who at the bridge would be first to fall,
Who that day would be Lying dead,
Pierced by a British musket-ball.

You know the rest. In books you have read,
How the British Regulars fired and fled,—
How the farmers gave them ball for ball,
From behind each fence and farmyard wall,
Chasing the redcoats down the lane,
Then crossing the fields to emerge again
Under the trees at the turn of the road,
And only pausing to fire and load.
So through the night rode Paul Revere;

And so through the night went his cry of alarm
To every Middlesex village and farm,—
A cry of defiance, and not of fear,
A voice in the darkness, a knock at the door,
And a word that shall echo for evermore!
For, borne on the night-wind of the Past,
Through all our history, to the last,
In the hour of darkness and peril and need,
The people will waken and listen to hear
The hurrying hoof-beats of that steed,
And the midnight message of Paul Revere.

—Henry Wadsworth Longfellow

CONCORD HYMN

Sung at the Completion of the Battle Monument, July 4, 1837

By the rude bridge that arched the flood,
  Their flag to April's breeze unfurled,
Here once the embattled farmers stood
  And fired the shot heard round the world.

The foe long since in silence slept;
  Alike the conqueror silent sleeps;
And Time the ruined bridge has swept
  Down the dark stream which seaward creeps.

On this green bank, by this soft stream,
  We set to-day a votive stone;
That memory may their deed redeem,
  When, like our sires, our sons are gone.

Spirit, that made those heroes dare
  To die and leave their children free,
Bid Time and Nature gently spare
  The shaft we raise to them and thee.

      —Ralph Waldo Emerson

"What They Fight About"

W ar is inherently a guy thing, caused by a bellicose gene that manifests itself the moment they hold a toy gun.

I once inadvertently engaged in a type of warfare that was disguised as a marriage and founded on the concept of M.A.D. (mutually assured destruction). When I finally ran up the white flag, the body count stood at three. I'm now a conscientious objector.

But real war involves men protecting and defending their place in life. An early warrior's chattel created the need for war. They'd return home after a tough day of clubbing each other senseless to the women and children who nurtured them.

But as tough as warfare was and is, it was always the bailiwick of men. And I know that most men don't like the idea that women now serve in the military. Who can blame them? If I lost one of my acrylic nails on the battlefield, I'd crawl back through a minefield to retrieve it, risking the lives of my whole platoon while re-affixing it. Television has changed the face of war, and there's no way I'd be seen on camera holding a rifle with a broken nail.

And forget defoliating agents. Too harsh. Seems a good depilatory for legs would work just as well. And depth charges? Turn on the Jacuzzi jets, please.

We've tried to mainstream war. The 1960s saw a prolifera-tion of war toys, with GI Joe as the king, a plastic icon for little boys. But c'mon! When that guy takes to wearing an earring like his civilian pal, Ken, we might see the first insurrection on American soil. Or maybe it'd be a "Million-Man Skip" through Washington.

Without the threat of war on our shores since the Civil War, our leaders have sought battles elsewhere. In the '60s we drafted boys right out of high school and parachuted them into Asian jungles they couldn't even find on a map. It was war for them, a "police action" for those who sent them.

I think we'd be vastly disappointed in a war in the United States. What have we got to fight about, and who's going to invade us? Mexico taught us a lesson at the Alamo. And Canadians don't know a gun from a rake. Guess there's always Miami, but damn if I want to be at war with soldiers wearing huaraches.

OK, fellas, let's get real honest about this war thing. Big three reasons you'd go today: you get to wear big black combat boots; you and the PMS (postal mind set) guys can carry the same assault weapons; and you know damn well that women love a man in uniform. I am no exception. Even a UPS delivery man is not safe around me.

Many of the following poems depict war as it once was, with chivalry and honor. Lovelace, the chump, dumps his girlfriend Lucasta for the privilege of going to battle, while Service offers a unique POW scenario that is the ultimate in catch-and-release. Then there's Brautigan, who puts it all in perspective with his take on Vietnam.

Oh, and I guess the editor thought I wouldn't notice, but there was a glaring omission of any verse related to the 1865 War of Northern Aggression. Doesn't the name DIXIE mean anything to him?

— kgs

Editor's note: Get over it.

THE CHARGE OF THE LIGHT BRIGADE

Half a league, half a league,
Half a league onward,
All in the valley of Death
    Rode the six hundred.
"Forward the Light Brigade!
Charge for the guns!" he said.
Into the valley of Death
    Rode the six hundred.

"Forward, the Light Brigade!"
Was there a man dismayed?
Not though the soldier knew
    Someone had blundered.
Theirs not to make reply,
Theirs not to reason why,
Theirs but to do and die.
Into the valley of Death
    Rode the six hundred.

Cannon to right of them,
Cannon to left of them,
Cannon in front of them
    Volleyed and thundered;
Stormed at with shot and shell,
Boldly they rode and well,
Into the jaws of Death,
Into the mouth of hell
    Rode the six hundred.

Flashed all their sabres bare,
Flashed as they turned in air
Sabring the gunners there,
Charging an army, while
    All the world wondered.
Plunged in the battery-smoke
Right through the line they broke;
Cossack and Russian
Reeled from the sabre-stroke
    Shattered and sundered.
Then they rode back, but not,
    Not the six hundred.

Cannon to right of them,
Cannon to left of them,
Cannon behind them
    Volleyed and thundered;
Stormed at with shot and shell,
While horse and hero fell.
They that had fought so well
Came through the jaws of Death,
Back from the mouth of hell,
All that was left of them,
    Left of six hundred.

When can their glory fade?
O the wild charge they made!
    All the world wondered.
Honor the charge they made!
Honor the Light Brigade,
    Noble six hundred!

—Alfred, Lord Tennyson

THE MARCH OF THE DEAD

The cruel war was over—oh, the triumph was so sweet!
　　We watched the troops returning, through our tears;
There was triumph, triumph, triumph down the scarlet glittering
　　　　street,
　　And you scarce could hear the music for the cheers.
And you scarce could see the house-tops for the flags that flew
　　　　between;
　　The bells were pealing madly to the sky;
And everyone was shouting for the Soldiers of the Queen,
　　And the glory of an age was passing by.

And then there came a shadow, swift and sudden, dark and drear;
　　The bells were silent, not an echo stirred.
The flags were drooping sullenly, the men forgot to cheer;
　　We waited, and we never spoke a word.
The sky grew darker, darker, till from out the gloomy rack
　　There came a voice that checked the heart with dread:
"Tear down, tear down your bunting now, and hang up sable
　　　　black;
　　They are coming—it's the Army of the Dead."

They were coming, they were coming, gaunt and ghastly, sad and
　　　　slow;
　　They were coming, all the crimson wrecks of pride;
With faces seared, and cheeks red smeared, and haunting eyes of
　　　　woe,
　　And clotted holes the khaki couldn't hide.
Oh, the clammy brow of anguish! the livid, foam-flecked lips!
　　The reeling ranks of ruin swept along!
The limb that trailed, the hand that failed, the bloody finger tips!
　　And oh, the dreary rhythm of their song!

"They left us on the veldt-side, but we felt we couldn't stop
  On this, our England's crowning festal day;
We're the men of Magersfontein, we're the men of Spion Kop,
  Colenso—we're the men who had to pay.
We're the men who paid the blood-price. Shall the grave be all
      our gain?
  You owe us. Long and heavy is the score.
Then cheer us for our glory now, and cheer us for our pain,
  And cheer us as ye never cheered before."

The folks were white and stricken, and each tongue seemed
      weighted with lead;
  Each heart was clutched in hollow hand of ice;
And every eye was staring at the horror of the dead,
  The pity of the men who paid the price.
They were come, were come to mock us, in the first flush of our
      peace;
  Through writhing lips their teeth were all agleam;
They were coming in their thousands—oh, would they never
      cease!
  I closed my eyes, and then—it was a dream.

There was triumph, triumph, triumph down the scarlet
      gleaming street;
  The town was mad; a man was like a boy.
A thousand flags were flaming where the sky and city meet;
  A thousand bells were thundering the joy.
There was music, mirth and sunshine; but some eyes shone
      with regret;
  And while we stun with cheers our homing braves,
O God, in Thy great mercy, let us nevermore forget
  The graves they left behind, the bitter graves.

— Robert Service

TO LUCASTA, GOING TO THE WARS

Tell me not, Sweet, I am unkind
    That from the nunnery
Of thy chaste breast and quiet mind,
    To war and arms I fly.

True, a new mistress now I chase,
    The first foe in the field;
And with a stronger faith embrace
    A sword, a horse, a shield.

Yet this inconstancy is such
    As you too shall adore;
I could not love thee, Dear, so much,
    Loved I not Honour more.

            — Richard Lovelace

MY PRISONER

We was in a crump-'ole, 'im and me;
Fightin' wiv our bayonets was we;
Fightin' 'ard as 'ell we was,
Fightin' fierce as fire because
It was 'im or me as must be downed;
'E was twice as big as me;
I was 'arf the weight of 'e;
We was like a terryer and a 'ound.

'Struth! But 'e was sich a 'andsome bloke.
Me, I'm 'andsome as a chunk o' coke.
Did I give it 'im? Not 'arf!
Why, it fairly made me laugh,
'Cos 'is bloomin' bellows wasn't sound.
Couldn't fight for monkey nuts.
Soon I gets 'im in the guts,
There 'e lies a-floppin' on the ground.

In I goes to finish up the job.
Quick 'e throws 'is 'ands above 'is nob;
Speakin' English good as me:
"'Tain't no use to kill," says 'e;
"Can't yer tyke me prisoner instead?"
"Why, I'd like to, sir," says I;
"But—yer knows the reason why:
If we pokes our noses out we're dead.

"Sorry, sir. Then on the other 'and
(As a gent like you must understand),
If I 'olds you longer 'ere,
Wiv yer pals so werry near,

It's me 'oo'll 'ave a free trip to Berlin;
If I lets yer go away,
Why, you'll fight another day:
See the sitooation I am in.

"Anyway I'll tell you wot I'll do,
Bein' kind and seein' as it's you,
Knowin' 'ow it's cold, the feel
Of a 'alf a yard o' steel,
I'll let yer 'ave a rifle ball instead;
Now, jist think yerself in luck . . .
'Ere, ol' man! You keep 'em stuck,
Them saucy dooks o' yours, above yer 'ead."

'Ow 'is mits shot up it made me smile!
'Ow 'e seemed to ponder for a while!
Then 'e says: "It seems a shyme,
Me, a man wot's known ter Fyme:
Give me blocks of stone, I'll give yer gods.
Whereas, pardon me, I'm sure
You, my friend, are still obscure . . ."
"In war," says I, "that makes no blurry odds."

Then says 'e: "I've painted picters too . . .
Oh, dear God! The work I planned to do,
And to think this is the end!"
"'Ere," says I, "my hartist friend,
Don't you give yerself no friskin' airs.
Picters, statoos, is that why
You should be let off to die?
That the best ye done? Just say yer prayers."

Once again 'e seems ter think awhile.
Then 'e smiles a werry 'aughty smile:
"Why, no, sir, it's not the best;
There's a locket next me breast,
Picter of a gel 'oo's eyes are blue.
That's the best I've done," says 'e.
"That's me darter, aged three . . ."
"Blimy!" says I, "I've a nipper, too."

Straight I chucks my rifle to one side;
Shows 'im wiv a lovin' farther's pride
Me own little Mary Jane.
Proud 'e shows me 'is Elaine,
And we talks as friendly as can be;
Then I 'elps 'im on 'is way,
'Opes 'e's sife at 'ome to-day,
Wonders—*'ow would 'e have treated me?*

— Robert Service

"STAR-SPANGLED" NAILS

You've got
some "Star-Spangled"
    nails
in your coffin, kid.
That's what
they've done for you,
    son.

— Richard Brautigan

DANNY DEEVER

"What are the bugles blowin' for?" said Files-on-Parade.
"To turn you out, to turn you out," the Color-Sergeant said.
"What makes you look so white, so white?" said Files-on-
    Parade.
"I'm dreadin' what I've got to watch," the Color-Sergeant said.
    For they're hangin' Danny Deever, you can hear the Dead
        March play,
    The Regiment's in 'ollow square—they're hangin' him
        today;
    They've taken of his buttons off an' cut his stripes away,
An' they're hangin' Danny Deever in the mornin'.

"What makes the rear-rank breathe so 'ard?" said Files-on-
    Parade.
"It's bitter cold, it's bitter cold," the Color-Sergeant said.
"What makes that front-rank man fall down?" said Files-on-
    Parade.
"A touch o' sun, a touch o' sun," the Color-Sergeant said.
    They are hangin' Danny Deever, they are marchin' of 'im
        round.
    They 'ave 'alted Danny Deever by 'is coffin on the ground;
    And 'e'll swing in 'arf a minute for a sneakin' shootin'
        hound—
O they're hangin' Danny Deever in the mornin'!

"'Is cot was right-'and cot to mine," said Files-on-Parade.
"'E's sleepin' out an' far tonight," the Color-Sergeant said.
"I've drunk 'is beer a score o' times," said Files-on-Parade.
"'E's drinkin' bitter beer alone," the Color-Sergeant said.
    They are hangin' Danny Deever, you must mark 'im to 'is
        place,

For 'e shot a comrade sleepin'—you must look 'im in the
    face;
  Nine 'undred of 'is county an' the Regiment's disgrace.
While they're hangin' Danny Deever in the mornin'.

"What's that so black agin the sun?" said Files-on-Parade.
"It's Danny fightin' 'ard for life," the Color-Sergeant said.
"What's that that whimpers over'ead?" said Files-on-Parade.
"It's Danny's soul that's passin' now," the Color-Sergeant said.
    For they're done with Danny Deever, you can 'ear the quick-
      step play,
    The Regiment's in column, an' they're marchin' us away;
    Ho! the young recruits are shakin', an' they'll want their
      beer today,
After hangin' Danny Deever in the mornin'!

— Rudyard Kipling

OLD IRONSIDES

Ay, tear her tattered ensign down!
Long has it waved on high,
And many an eye has danced to see
That banner in the sky;
Beneath it rung the battle shout,
And burst the cannon's roar;—
The meteor of the ocean air
Shall sweep the clouds no more!

Her deck, once red with heroes' blood,
Where knelt the vanquished foe,
When winds were hurrying o'er the flood,
And waves were white below,
No more shall feel the victor's tread,
Or know the conquered knee;—
The harpies of the shore shall pluck
The eagle of the sea!

O, better that her shattered hulk
Should sink beneath the wave;
Her thunders shook the mighty deep,
And there should be her grave;
Nail to the mast her holy flag,
Set every threadbare sail,
And give her to the god of storms,
The lightning and the gale!

— Oliver Wendell Holmes

THE CONVALESCENT

. . . So I walked among the willows very quietly all night;
there was no moon at all, at all; no timid star alight;
There was no light at all, at all; I wint from tree to tree,
And I called him as his mother called, but he nivver answered me.

Oh I called him all the night-time, as I walked the wood alone;
And I listened and I listened, but I nivver heard a moan;
Then I found him at the dawnin', when the sorry sky was red:
I was lookin' for the livin', but I only found the dead.

Sure I know that it was Shamus by the silver cross he wore;
But the bugles they were callin', and I heard the cannon roar.
Oh I had no time to tarry, so I said a little prayer,
And I clasped his hands together, and I left him lyin' there.

Now the birds are singin', singin', and I'm home in Donegal,
And it's Springtime, and I'm thinkin' that I only dreamed it all;
I dreamed about that evil wood, all crowded with its dead,
Where I knelt beside me brother when the battle-dawn was red.

Where I prayed beside me brother ere I wint to fight anew:
Such dreams as these are evil dreams; I can't believe it's true.
Where all is love and laughter, sure it's hard to think of loss . . .
But mother's sayin' nothin', and she clasps—*a silver cross.*

— Robert Service

A POISON TREE

I was angry with my friend:
I told my wrath, my wrath did end.
I was angry with my foe:
I told it not, my wrath did grow.

And I water'd it in fears,
Night and morning with my tears;
And I sunned it with smiles,
And with soft deceitful wiles.

And it grew both day and night,
Till it bore an apple bright;
And my foe beheld it shine,
And he knew that it was mine,

And into my garden stole
When the night had veil'd the pole;
In the morning glad I see
My foe outstretch'd beneath the tree.

— William Blake

THE CALL

(France, August first, 1914)

Far and near, high and clear,
Hark to the call of War!
Over the gorse and the golden dells,
Ringing and swinging of clamorous bells,
Praying and saying of wild farewells:
War! War! War!

High and low, all must go:
Hark to the shout of War!
Leave to the women the harvest yield;
Gird ye, men, for the sinister field;
A sabre instead of a scythe to wield:
War! Red War!

Rich and poor, lord and boor,
Hark to the blast of War!
Tinker and tailor and millionaire,
Actor in triumph and priest in prayer,
Comrades now in the hell out there,
Sweep to the fire of War!

Prince and page, sot and sage,
Hark to the roar of War!
Poet, professor and circus clown,
Chimney-sweeper and fop o' the town,
Into the pot and be melted down:
Into the pot of War!

Women all, hear the call,
The pitiless call of War!
Look your last on your dearest ones
Brothers and husbands, fathers, sons:
Swift they go to the ravenous guns,
The gluttonous guns of War.

Everywhere thrill the air
The maniac bells of War.
There will be little of sleeping to-night;
There will be wailing and weeping to-night;
Death's red sickle is reaping to-night:
War! War! War!

— Robert Service

GRASS

Pile the bodies high at Austerlitz and Waterloo.
Shovel them under and let me work—
I am the grass; I cover all.

And pile them high at Gettysburg
And pile them high at Ypres and Verdun.
Shovel them under and let me work.
Two years, ten years, and passengers ask the conductor:
What place is this?
Where are we now?

I am the grass.
Let me work.

— Carl Sandburg

"How They Angst"

><+>--O--<+>-<

A re men really all about true grit? I don't think so.

If all the world's a stage and we are but actors on it, guys are the barking seal act with an encore of spinning plates. But don't tell them, for God's sake. After all, they have an image to protect and a legend to uphold. Far be it from me to hint that they weren't jousting in a suit of armor next to Lancelot in a former life.

Frankly, it's their armor that I think it's all about.

Guys, take it off, all off! Don't be afraid to show us who you are! You might be surprised to see that we like you in spite of yourselves.

Besides, where has being an impenetrable, tough guy gotten you, oh ye of few words, closed minds, harnessed emotions, and too few tears? The grand prize is contrived relationships with fathers and sons, uneasy ones with daughters and mothers, and a tenuous one with wives.

It would be nice if today's guy could indeed be a lone wolf in sheep's clothing, a costume he could don at random. But alas, their "Y" chromosome creates an innate code of conduct. Thus they arrive on the scene, born to an ascribed role to protect, provide, and decide.

But part of the script they're handed is being rewritten. Recent social trends have caused a blurring of gender roles — a feminization of males — as an increasing number of women enter the workplace and more men choose or are channeled into non-traditional roles.

Is man's inner-child warrior psyche being threatened? Lots of guys certainly think so. And who can blame them? Hell, gender roles are so screwed up now, there's some geek with a perpetual smile writing books and giving seminars about men and women being from two different planets. So let's orbit!

It's a shame that guys are actualized through their jobs, that money equates to success and that peer pressure within one's caste system dictates the economics. Some guys are programmed to wear a tie and make the pretense of going to an office, even if it's selling Slim Jims at a convenience store.

But, boys, boys, go easy on yourselves. Don't let money become a substitute for work-related brawn. Where will women go to have their egos boosted if not to stroll beneath a 20-floor scaffolding? We must have workers in hard hats and tank tops to supply us with catcalls. I only ask that if it's really obscene, please yell in Spanish, although I'm not offended by the accompanying clucking and cacophony of whirring bird noises.

With all the credos associated with today's male gender, it appears that men may not really be in control of their own destinies. Regardless of how they see themselves, it seems they're on a treadmill with no "stop" button. How many dream of jumping off and saying "screw it"? But their role is so ingrained, most can't afford to question the alternatives.

So guys, turn the page and celebrate whomever you deem yourselves to be. There are no correct answers. Just keep your eyes on your own paper.

—kgs

THE ROAD NOT TAKEN

Two roads diverged in a yellow wood,
And sorry I could not travel both
And be one traveler, long I stood
And looked down one as far as I could
To where it bent in the undergrowth;

Then took the other, as just as fair,
And having perhaps the better claim,
Because it was grassy and wanted wear;
Though as for that the passing there
Had worn them really about the same,

And both that morning equally lay
In leaves no step had trodden black.
Oh, I kept the first for another day!
Yet knowing how way leads on to way,
I doubted if I should ever come back.

I shall be telling this with a sigh
Somewhere ages and ages hence:
Two roads diverged in a wood, and I—
I took the one less traveled by,
And that has made all the difference.

— Robert Frost

THE MEN THAT DON'T FIT IN

There is a race of men that don't fit in,
    A race that can't stay still;
So they break the hearts of kith and kin,
    And they roam the world at will.
They range the field and they rove the flood,
    And they climb the mountain's crest;
Theirs is the curse of the gypsy blood,
    And they don't know how to rest.

If they just went straight they might go far;
    They are strong and brave and true;
But they're always tired of the things that are,
    And they want the strange and new.
They say: "Could I find my proper groove,
    What a deep mark I would make!"
So they chop and change, and each fresh move
    Is only a fresh mistake.

And each forgets, as he strips and runs
    With a brilliant, fitful pace,
It's the steady, quiet, plodding ones
    Who win in the lifelong race.
And each forgets that his youth has fled,
    Forgets that his prime is past,
Till he stands one day, with a hope that's dead,
    In the glare of the truth at last.

He has failed, he has failed; he has missed his chance;
    He has just done things by half.
Life's been a jolly good joke on him,
    And now is the time to laugh.
Ha, ha! He is one of the Legion Lost;
    He was never meant to win;
He's a rolling stone, and it's bred in the bone;
    He's a man who won't fit in.

                — Robert Service

A MAN SAID TO THE UNIVERSE

A man said to the universe:
"Sir, I exist!"
"However," replied the universe,
"The fact has not created in me
A sense of obligation."

                — Stephen Crane

WHERE THE BLUE LOOPS CROSS

But then come nights like this
when the bedroom fan hums,
Judy chirps from her deep dream
and I fear sleep and the end
of our placid lives; thus, longing
for the Island of So What,
I beach myself in the T.V. room
where the blue glow of 1:27
on the VCR could just as well be
the glint on a Caribbean permit fish
flashing through the mangrove roots
of tidal flats. This aging, naked pod
of a body I carry now more slowly,
awkwardly, somehow reminds me less of that
than a fat goldfish I once saw
in a bowl on a doilied table
of a childhood friend. I was stunned
at the separateness of its small globe,
refracting a shimmer of sun while
reflecting that gold right there
over the crocheting of a Sunday morning.
Yet with all of that awe, the damn thing
trailed a frayed string of dung
around its tentative cosmos.
I'm forty, probably more than half done
if I'm not done tomorrow and am tempted
right now to cut a rough hole
in the roof, domesticate the constellations
in my own half-baked way, and yes,
awaken my sons, drag them under
the ragged hole and say "Chris, Max,

some day this will all be yours,"
pointing out lines between new stars
and supernovas: "And there my sons
is Toro, the Lawn Mower. And right
next to it, with Venus at the tip,
Judy, who in the legend drew a face
on a penis and starred it in a puppet show.
And farthest of all—there where
the twinkling dims—is a failure
of the imagination so immense that
I choose to call it Greg the Goldfish,
trailing its frazzled aspirations toward
the established credibilities of Cancer."
Of course I will wake no one up, I will
cut no hole, name no constellations.
The blue permit flashes again
as I move my toe. It's 2:04
here on the Island of So What.
I gave up looking for passing freighters
years ago—or tramping out SOS
in footprints for the occasional jet.
I drank the only bottle of whisky
and corked in it a dollar bill
with this inscription:
"In spite of all this, I still love you,"
and even then, checking the wind,
currents and tides for the best drift
like a Polynesian sailor,
I've found that bottle again and again,
bumping against one shore or another
here at the juncture of the infinite
where the blue loops cross, terminating 2:28.

— Greg Keeler

DECEMBER 30

At 1:03 in the morning a fart
smells like a marriage between
an avocado and a fish head.

I have to get out of bed
to write this down without
    my glasses on.

           — Richard Brautigan

THE QUITTER

When you're lost in the Wild, and you're scared as a child,
    And Death looks you bang in the eye,
And you're sore as a boil, it's according to Hoyle
    To cock your revolver and . . . die.
But the Code of a Man says: "Fight all you can,"
    And self-dissolution is barred.
In hunger and woe, oh, it's easy to blow . . .
    It's the hell-served-for-breakfast that's hard.

"You're sick of the game!" Well, now, that's a shame.
    You're young and you're brave and you're bright.
"You've had a raw deal!" I know—but don't squeal,
    Buck up, do your damnedest, and fight.
It's the plugging away that will win you the day,
    So don't be a piker, old pard!
Just draw on your grit; it's so easy to quit:
    It's the keeping-your-chin-up that's hard.

It's easy to cry that you're beaten—and die;
    It's easy to crawfish and crawl;
But to fight and to fight when hope's out of sight—
    Why, that's the best game of them all!
And though you come out of each gruelling bout,
    All broken and beaten and scarred,
Just have one more try—it's dead easy to die,
    It's the keeping-on-living that's hard.

— Robert Service

HOMAGE TO LOUIS L'AMOUR

That hunk who rode off
into the sunset and said
he was never coming back
but he always did—
you know—the one who wore
a white hat at first but
then started wearing
a black hat—the one who had
a big pig of a Colt
sticking out in front of him
when things got a little vague?
Well, he's *not* coming back.
First the hat got so dark
you couldn't even see it.
Then the Colt started to jam.
Then the hunk and his horse
got into aerobics—
jazzercise to be exact.
They started to
feel good about themselves.
When the cattlemen and sheepmen
shot it out at the edge of town,
he served as a go-between,
telling first one side
then the other,
"I like what you're saying,"
or "I'm hearing you—
would you go with that?"
till the calf lay down
with the lamb.

— Greg Keeler

THE SONG OF THE WAGE-SLAVE

When the long, long day is over, and the Big Boss gives me my
    pay,
I hope that it won't be hell-fire, as some of the parsons say.
And I hope that it won't be heaven, with some of the parsons
    I've met—
All I want is just quiet, just to rest and forget.
Look at my face, toil-furrowed; look at my calloused hands;
Master, I've done Thy bidding, wrought in Thy many lands—
Wrought for the little masters, big-bellied they be, and rich;
I've done their desire for a daily hire, and I die like a dog in a
    ditch.
I have used the strength Thou hast given, Thou knowest I did
    not shirk;
Threescore years of labor—Thine be the long day's work.
And now, Big Master, I'm broken and bent and twisted and
    scarred,
But I've held my job, and Thou knowest, and Thou will not
    judge me hard.
Thou knowest my sins are many, and often I've played the
    fool—
Whiskey and cards and women, they made me the devil's tool.
I was just like a child with money; I flung it away with a curse,
Feasting a fawning parasite, or glutting a harlot's purse;
Then back to the woods repentant, back to the mill or the
    mine,
I, the worker of workers, everything in my line.
Everything hard but headwork (I'd no more brains than a kid),
A brute with brute strength to labor, doing as I was bid;
Living in camps with men-folk, a lonely and loveless life;
Never knew kiss of sweetheart, never caress of wife
A brute with brute strength to labor, and they were so far
    above—

Yet I'd gladly have gone to the gallows for one little look of
    Love.
I, with the strength of two men, savage and shy and wild—
Yet how I'd ha' treasured a woman, and the sweet, warm kiss of
    a child!
Well, 'tis Thy world, and Thou knowest I blaspheme and my
    ways be rude;
But I've lived my life as I found it, and I've done my best to be
    good;
I, the primitive toiler, half naked and grimed to the eyes,
Sweating it deep in their ditches, swining it stark in their sties;
Hurling down forests before me, spanning tumultuous streams;
Down in the ditch building o'er me palaces fairer than dreams;
Boring the rock to the ore-bed, driving the road through the fen,
Resolute, dumb, uncomplaining, a man in a world of men.
Master, I've filled my contract, wrought in Thy many lands;
Not by my sins wilt Thou judge me, but by the work of my
    hands.
Master, I've done Thy bidding, and the light is low in the west,
And the long, long shift is over . . . Master, I've earned it—
Rest.

— Robert Service

THE WINOS ON POTRERO HILL

Alas, they get
their bottles
from a small
neighborhood store.
The old Russian
sells them port
and passes no moral
judgment. They go
and sit under
the green bushes
that grow along
the wooden stairs.
They could almost
be exotic flowers,
they drink so
quietly.

— Richard Brautigan

ACQUAINTED WITH THE NIGHT

I have been one acquainted with the night.
I have walked out in rain—and back in rain.
I have outwalked the furthest city light.

I have looked down the saddest city lane.
I have passed by the watchman on his beat
And dropped my eyes, unwilling to explain.

I have stood still and stopped the sound of feet
When far away an interrupted cry
Came over houses from another street,

But not to call me back or say good-by;
And further still at an unearthly height
One luminary clock against the sky

Proclaimed the time was neither wrong nor right.
I have been one acquainted with the night.

— Robert Frost

AUTOMATIC ANTHOLE

Driven by hunger, I had another
forced bachelor dinner tonight.
I had a lot of trouble making
up my mind whether to eat Chinese
food or have a hamburger. God,
I hate eating dinner alone. It's
      like being dead.

— Richard Brautigan

THE SCEPTIC

My Father Christmas passed away
When I was barely seven.
At twenty-one, alack-a-day,
I lost my hope of heaven.

Yet not in either lies the curse:
The hell of it's because
I don't know which loss hurt the worse—
My God or Santa Claus.

— Robert Service

CHICKADEE DEJECTION

The car won't start,
the pipes all freeze,
but I step out to get
the morning paper,
my wet hair freezing
into a helmet,
and see a bush full
of sonofabitching
chickadees.
Who the hell
do they think they are
to cheep and peck seeds,
to shit their little
chickadee shit
when the Earth could
just as well be
one of Neptune's moons?
Here, take the
goddamn newspaper.
Whatever the news is,
it's wrong.

— Greg Keeler

"Whatever Turns Them On"

⊱─┤◆⟩─○─⟨◆├─⊰

Inspiration, that elusive brainstorm one prays for but which usually visits unannounced at 3 a.m. And as you'll read, it arrives for poets in the midst of certain epiphanies — some divine, others more mundane, nevertheless, all sincere and cathartic.

But shift your thoughts of inspiration away from poets to the profane, secular realm and this tool of creative muse manifests itself differently.

Ask today's guy on the street, "What inspires you?" You might hear, "My wife and her Visa bill. She has a black belt in shopping and after I finally paid the thing off, they retired her credit card numbers."

Well, I'll accept financial stimulus to a degree, but throughout history, whether it's a case of love, hate or indifference, men have been inspired by women more than they care to admit.

Indeed, women are able to spark a man's genius, assuming that's what it really is. Inspiration can often be the startling byproduct of the unexpected. And there are plenty of examples. Lest we forget John Bobbit, who was inspired to become a film star after he had a sensitive part of his anatomy sliced off by his wife, Lorena. Emulating the style of a former film monster, he opted for Boris Karloff's zipper-stitch during his surgical reattachment and got the role as the protagonist in *Frankenpenis* .

James Hinkley was so inspired by actress Jodie Foster that he tried to get her attention by shooting President Ronald Reagan. She was not impressed.

Then there are the romantic British monarchs. King George VIII abdicated his throne for the woman he loved, Wallis Simpson, an American divorcee who inspired the short-term king to say "take this job and shove it" so he could downgrade to duke and stand around in a smoking jacket, playing Frisbee with his dogs. Wow, what a woman!

And there's Prince Charles and his paramour Camilla, who make the Duke and Duchess of Windsor look like a geriatric Ken and Barbie. I don't know what Camilla has, other than looking like Mr. Ed with cleavage, but she inspired Charles to leave his wife, which has left his ascension to the throne shaky.

So it seems that inspiration has many faces, including one that launched a thousand ships, which I truly hope didn't refer to Kathie Lee Gifford and the Carnival Cruise Line.

The poems that follow gather inspiration from many sources, not all of them women. Langston Hughes revels in the tranquility of rivers; Robert Service heeds the call of the wild; and Edwin A. Robinson's poem, "Richard Cory," reminds us that wealth may not be a blessing but, instead, a curse. Or as satirist Dorothy Parker said, "If you want to know what God thinks of money, look who He gives it to."

—kgs

RICHARD CORY

Whenever Richard Cory went down town,
We people on the pavement looked at him:
He was a gentleman from sole to crown,
Clean favored, and imperially slim.

And he was always quietly arrayed,
And he was always human when he talked;
But still he fluttered pulses when he said,
"Good-morning," and he glittered when he walked.

And he was rich—yes, richer than a king—
And admirably schooled in every grace:
In fine, we thought that he was everything
To make us wish that we were in his place.

So on we worked, and waited for the light,
And went without the meat, and cursed the bread;
And Richard Cory, one calm summer night,
Went home and put a bullet through his head.

    — Edwin Arlington Robinson

ADRENALIN MOTHER

Adrenalin Mother,
with your dress of comets
and shoes of swift bird wings
and shadow of jumping fish,
thank you for touching,
understanding and loving my life.
Without you, I am dead.

    — Richard Brautigan

A DIALOGUE BETWEEN THE SOUL AND BODY

SOUL:
 O who shall from this dungeon raise
A soul enslaved so many ways?
With bolts of bones, that fettered stands
In feet; and manacled in hands:
Here blinded with an eye; and there
Deaf with the drumming of an ear;
A soul hung up, as 'twere, in chains
Of nerves, and arteries, and veins;
Tortured, besides each other part,
In a vain head and double heart.

BODY:
 O who shall me deliver whole
From bonds of this tyrannic soul?
Which, stretched upright, impales me so
That mine own precipice I go;
And warms and moves this needless frame
(A fever could but do the same);
And, wanting where its spite to try,
Has made me live to let me die;
A body that could never rest,
Since this ill spirit it possessed.

SOUL:
     What magic could me thus confine
Within another's grief to pine?
Where whatsoever it complain,
I feel, that cannot feel, the pain.
And all my care itself employs
That to preserve, which me destroys;
Constrained not only to endure
Diseases, but, what's worse, the cure;
And ready oft the port to gain,
Am shipwrecked into health again.

BODY:
     But physic yet could never reach
The maladies thou me dost teach:
Whom first the cramp of hope does tear;
And then the palsy shakes of fear;
The pestilence of love does heat;
Or hatred's hidden ulcer eat;
Joy's cheerful madness does perplex,
Or sorrow's other madness vex;
Which knowledge forces me to know,
And memory will not forgo.
What but a soul could have the wit
To build me up for sin so fit?
So architects do square and hew
Green trees that in the forest grew.

              — Andrew Marvell

TO ALTHEA, FROM PRISON

When Love with unconfined wings
    Hovers within my gates,
And my divine Althea brings
    To whisper at the grates;
When I lie tangled in her hair
    And fetter'd to her eye,
The birds that wanton in the air
    Know no such liberty.

When flowing cups run swiftly round
    With no allaying Thames,
Our careless heads with roses bound,
    Our hearts with loyal flames;
When thirsty grief in wine we steep,
    When healths and draughts go free—
Fishes that tipple in the deep
    Know no such liberty.

When, like committed linnets, I
    With shriller throat shall sing
The sweetness, mercy, majesty,
    And glories of my King;
When I shall voice aloud how good
    He is, how great should be,
Enlarged winds, that curl the flood,
    Know no such liberty.

Stone walls do not a prison make,
    Nor iron bars a cage;
Minds innocent and quiet take
    That for an hermitage;

If I have freedom in my love
    And in my soul am free,
Angels alone, that soar above,
    Enjoy such liberty.

          — Richard Lovelace

THE NEGRO SPEAKS OF RIVERS

I've known rivers:
I've known rivers ancient as the world and older than the flow
    of human blood in human veins.

My soul has grown deep like the rivers.

I bathed in the Euphrates when dawns were young.
I built my hut near the Congo and it lulled me to sleep.

I looked upon the Nile and raised the pyramids above it.
I heard the singing of the Mississippi when Abe Lincoln went
    down to New Orleans, and I've seen its muddy bosom turn
    all golden in the sunset.

I've known rivers:
Ancient, dusky rivers.

My soul has grown deep like the rivers.

          — Langston Hughes

THE LURE OF LITTLE VOICES

There's a cry from out the loneliness—oh, listen, Honey, listen!
    Do you hear it, do you fear it, you're a-holding of me so?
You're a-sobbing in your sleep, dear, and your lashes, how they
    glisten—
    Do you hear the Little Voices all a-begging me to go?

All a-begging me to leave you. Day and night they're pleading,
    praying,
    On the North-wind, on the West-wind, from the peak and
    from the plain;
Night and day they never leave me—do you know what they are
    saying?
    "He was ours before you got him, and we want him once
    again."

Yes, they're wanting me, they're haunting me, the awful lonely
    places;
    They're whining and they're whimpering as if each had a
    soul;
They're calling from the wilderness, the vast and God-like
    spaces,
    The stark and sullen solitudes that sentinel the Pole.

They miss my little camp-fires, ever brightly, bravely gleaming
    In the womb of desolation, where was never man before;
As comradeless I sought them, lion-hearted, loving, dreaming,
    And they hailed me as a comrade, and they loved me ever-
    more.

And now they're all a-crying, and it's no use me denying;
    The spell of them is on me and I'm helpless as a child;
My heart is aching, aching, but I hear them, sleeping, waking;
    It's the Lure of Little Voices, it's the mandate of the Wild.

I'm afraid to tell you, Honey, I can take no bitter leaving;
    But softly in the sleep-time from your love I'll steal away.
Oh, it's cruel, dearie, cruel, and it's God knows how I'm
      grieving;
    But His loneliness is calling, and He knows I must obey.

                    — Robert Service

"How They Grieve"

D o men grieve over misspent youth? Depends on what they spent it on, I suppose. The poets included here illustrate men's propensity to hitch a ride on life's winged chariot. However, they were remiss in not mentioning the stages of male senility. So I'll do it for them. First they forget names; then they forget faces; next they forget to zip up; and, finally, they forget to zip down. Women, by comparison, have selective memory loss and choose when and what to forget.

Middle-aged men seem to become very introspective and question everything about themselves and what they stand for, feeling it important to leave some sort of legacy, evidence they really "were," and weren't just a rumor.

But did they just exist or really live? I think if they existed they left children and a good business. If they lived, they left a young wife with a body that could stop a New York cabbie.

Men exhibit their terror over aging by showing, not telling, us that they are a study in doubt and ego assailment. Many hire personal trainers, buy cars that go faster than their pacemakers, and some join the hair club.

Then there are the questions pertaining to their physical

appeal. Am I too young to be old or too old to be young? Do women find me attractive? Maybe I should trade the old gray mare in on a young filly. A brief note here to guys: Few women in this solar system are likely to find you, at middle age, an irresistible stud. But all is not lost. Throw in a Hermes scarf, a bauble from Bulgari, hand her a Judith Leiber bag and it's time to trip the light fantastic. There is a definite correlation between material enticement and love being blind.

Since our society is predicated on virility, a guy's mawkish display of sentiment isn't for public consumption. It's imperative that he preserve that macho visage, even if the five o'clock shadow he's working on looks more like a case of mange in its early stage. Frankly, I find a man unafraid to connect with his feminine side very sensual, as long as he doesn't borrow my underwear.

But my God, these aging men are so hung up about sex, apologizing all over themselves for not having the drive or staying power they did at twenty. Do they ever stop to think that perhaps women don't care, that maybe we'd prefer a quiet afternoon by a mountain stream, with an impassioned gentleman reciting poetry while we close our eyes and fantasize about the good old days and our twenty-year-old boyfriends?

I often wonder if men would trade old and wise for young and foolish. Any woman who says she wouldn't, hasn't taken estrogen yet.

Of the poems that follow, pay particular attention to bad boy Brautigan, who thumbs his nose at our culture obsessed with youth and beauty. In thumbing his nose at such superfluousness, he's warning you to not allow your spirit to precede you to the point where physical death becomes a moot point.

— kgs

THE SHOOTING OF DAN McGREW

A bunch of the boys were whooping it up in the Malamute
    saloon;
The kid that handles the music-box was hitting a jag-time tune;
Back of the bar, in a solo game, sat Dangerous Dan McGrew,
And watching his luck was his light-o'-love, the lady that's known
    as Lou.

When out of the night, which was fifty below, and into the din
    and the glare,
There stumbled a miner fresh from the creeks, dog-dirty, and
    loaded for bear.
He looked like a man with a foot in the grave and scarcely the
    strength of a louse,
Yet he tilted a poke of dust on the bar, and he called for drinks for
    the house.
There was none could place the stranger's face, though we
    searched ourselves for a clue;
But we drank his health, and the last to drink was Dangerous Dan
    McGrew.

There's men that somehow just grip you; yes, and hold them hard
    like a spell;
And such was he, and he looked to me like a man who had lived
    in hell;
With a face most hair, and the dreary stare of a dog whose day is
    done,
As he watered the green stuff in his glass, and the drops fell one
    by one.
Then I got to figgering who he was, and wondering what he'd do,
And I turned my head—and there watching him was the lady
    that's known as Lou.

His eyes went rubbering round the room, and he seemed in a
kind of daze,
Till at last that old piano fell in the way of his wandering gaze.
The rag-time kid was having a drink; there was no one else on the
stool,
So the stranger stumbles across the room, and flops down there
like a fool.
In a buckskin shirt that was glazed with dirt he sat, and I saw him
sway;
Then he clutched the keys with his talon hands—my God! but
that man could play.

Were you ever out in the Great Alone, when the moon was awful
clear,
And the icy mountains hemmed you in with a silence you most
could hear;
With only the howl of a timber wolf, and you camped there in the
cold,
A half-dead thing in a stark, dead world, clean mad for the muck
called gold;
While high overhead, green, yellow and red, the North Lights
swept in bars?—
Then you've a hunch what the music meant . . . hunger and night
and the stars.

And hunger not of the belly kind, that's banished with bacon and
beans,
But the gnawing hunger of lonely men for a home and all that it
means;
For a fireside far from the cares that are, four walls and a roof
above;
But oh! so cramful of cosy joy, and crowned with a woman's
love—

A woman dearer than all the world, and true as Heaven is true—
(God! how ghastly she looks through her rouge,—the lady that's
    known as Lou.)

Then on a sudden the music changed, so soft that you scarce
    could hear;
But you felt that your life had been looted clean of all that it once
    held dear;
That someone had stolen the woman you loved; that her love was
    a devil's lie;
That your guts were gone, and the best for you was to crawl away
    and die.
'Twas the crowning cry of a heart's despair, and it thrilled you
    through and through—
"I guess I'll make it a spread misere," said Dangerous Dan
    McGrew.

The music almost died away . . . then it burst like a pent-up
    flood;
And it seemed to say, "Repay, repay," and my eyes were blind
    with blood.
The thought came back of an ancient wrong, and it stung like a
    frozen lash,
And the lust awoke to kill, to kill . . . then the music stopped
    with a crash,
And the stranger turned, and his eyes they burned in a most
    peculiar way;
In a buckskin shirt that was glazed with dirt he sat, and I saw him
    sway;
Then his lips went in in a kind of grin, and he spoke, and his
    voice was calm,
And "Boys," says he, "you don't know me, and none of you care
    a damn;

But I want to state, and my words are straight, and I'll bet my
poke they're true,
That one of you is a hound of hell . . . and that one is Dan
McGrew."

Then I ducked my head, and the lights went out, and two guns
blazed in the dark,
And a woman screamed, and the lights went up, and two men
lay stiff and stark.
Pitched on his head, and pumped full of lead, was Dangerous
Dan McGrew,
While the man from the creeks lay clutched to the breast of the
lady that's known as Lou.

These are the simple facts of the case, and I guess I ought to
know.
They say that the stranger was crazed with "hooch," and I'm
not denying it's so.
I'm not so wise as the lawyer guys, but strictly between us
two—
The woman that kissed him and—pinched his poke—was the
lady that's known as Lou.

— Robert Service

DO NOT GO GENTLE INTO THAT GOOD NIGHT

Do not go gentle into that good night,
Old age should burn and rave at close of day;
Rage, rage against the dying of the light.

Though wise men at their end know dark is right,
Because their words had forked no lightning they
Do not go gentle into that good night.

Good men, the last wave by, crying how bright
Their frail deeds might have danced in a green bay,
Rage, rage against the dying of the light.

Wild men who caught and sang the sun in flight,
And learn, too late, they grieved it on its way,
Do not go gentle into that good night.

Grave men, near death, who see with blinding sight
Blind eyes could blaze like meteors and be gay,
Rage, rage against the dying of the light.

And you, my father, there on the sad height,
Curse, bless, me now with your fierce tears, I pray,
Do not go gentle into that good night.
Rage, rage against the dying of the light.

— Dylan Thomas

MY NOSE IS GROWING OLD

Yup.
A long lazy September look
in the mirror
say it's true:

I'm 31
and my nose is growing
    old.

It starts about 1/2
an inch
below the bridge
and strolls geriatrically
    down
for another inch or so:
    stopping.

Fortunately, the rest
of the nose is comparatively
    young.

I wonder if girls
will want me with an
    old nose.

I can hear them now
the heartless bitches

"He's cute
    but his nose
is old."

            — Richard Brautigan

I REMEMBER, I REMEMBER

I remember, I remember,
The house where I was born,
The little window where the sun
Came peeping in at morn;
He never came a wink too soon,
Nor brought too long a day,
But now, I often wish the night
Had borne my breath away!

I remember, I remember,
The roses, red and white,
The violets, and the lily-cups,
Those flowers made of light!
The lilacs where the robin built,
And where my brother set
The laburnum on his birthday,—
The tree is living yet!

I remember, I remember,
Where I was used to swing,
And thought the air must rush as fresh
To swallows on the wing;
My spirit flew in feathers then,
That is so heavy now,
And summer pools could hardly cool
The fever on my brow!

I remember, I remember
The fir trees dark and high;
I used to think their slender tops
Were close against the sky;

It was a childish ignorance,
 But now 'tis little joy
To know I'm farther off from Heaven
Than when I was a boy.

— Thomas Hood

BUFFALO BILL'S DEFUNCT

Buffalo Bill's
defunct
        who used to
ride a watersmooth-silver
                    stallion
and break onetwothreefourfive pigeonsjustlikethat
                                    Jesus
he was a handsome man
                    and what i want to know is
how do you like your blueeyed boy
Mister Death

— e.e. cummings

GRANDAD

Heaven's mighty sweet, I guess;
Ain't no rush to git there;
Been a sinner, more or less;
Maybe wouldn't fit there.
Wicked still, bound to confess;
Might jest pine a bit there.

Heaven's swell, the preachers say:
Got so used to earth here;
Had such good times all the way,
Frolic, fun and mirth here;
Eighty Springs ago to-day,
Since I had my birth here.

Quite a spell of happy years.
Wish I could begin it;
Cloud and sunshine, laughter, tears,
Livin' every minute.
Women, too, the pretty dears;
Plenty of 'em in it.

Heaven! that's another tale.
Mightn't let me chew there.
Gotta have me pot of ale;
Would I like the brew there?
Maybe I'd get slack and stale—
No more chores to do there.

Here I weed the garden plot,
Scare the crows from pillage;
Simmer in the sun a lot,

Talk about the tillage.
Yarn of battles I have fought,
Greybeard of the village.

Heaven's mighty fine, I know . . .
Still, it ain't so bad here.
See them maples all aglow;
Starlings seem so glad here:
I'll be mighty peeved to go,
Scrumptious times I've had here.

Lord, I know You'll understand.
With Your Light You'll lead me.
Though I'm not the pious brand,
I'm here when You need me.
Gosh! I know that Heaven's GRAND,
But dang it! God, *don't speed me.*

— Robert Service

AT THIRTY-FIVE

Three score and ten, the psalmist saith,
And half my course is well-nigh run;
I've had my flout at dusty death,
I've had my whack of feast and fun.
I've mocked at those who prate and preach;
I've laughed with any man alive;
But now with sobered heart I reach
The Great Divide of Thirty-five.

And looking back I must confess
I've little cause to feel elate.
 I've played the mummer more or less:
I fumbled fortune, flouted fate.
I've vastly dreamed and little done;
I've idly watched my brothers strive:
Oh, I have loitered in the sun
By primrose paths to Thirty-five!

And those who matched me in the race,
Well, some are out and trampled down;
The others jog with sober pace;
Yet one wins delicate renown.
O midnight feast and famished dawn!
O gay, hard life, with hope alive!
O golden youth, forever gone,
How sweet you seem at Thirty-five!

Each of our lives is just a book
As absolute as Holy Writ;
We humbly read, and may not look
Ahead, nor change one word of it

And here are joys and here are pains;
And here we fail and here we thrive;
O wondrous volume! what remains
When we reach chapter Thirty-five?

The very best, I dare to hope,
Ere Fate writes Finis to the tome;
A wiser head, a wider scope,
And for the gipsy heart, a home;
A songful home, with loved ones near,
With joy, with sunshine all alive
Watch me grow younger every year—
Old Age! thy name is Thirty-five!

— Robert Service

"What They Believe"

><del>+</del>◦<del>+</del>◁

There are no atheists in a foxhole or during an IRS audit. In fact, it's amazing how fast men call God's 800 number when disaster looms.

Unlike women, who unabashedly talk about God to anyone who won't slap them, men are much more circumspect and don't gush until they have a reason to. But once they start, you can't shut them up. Their conversion is so histrionic they must tell the world, "I was lost, but now I'm found!" Well, my attitude is be "found" somewhere else. It's old news to those of us who remember you in your pre-rapture days.

See, God has become more palatable to guys due to an updated PR (proselyte relations) campaign advocating His sanction of financial prosperity. Spiritual leaders are preaching the virtues of wealth as the conspicuous consumption of the 1980s melds into the rising spiritualism of the dawning Aquarian Age. And as we know, organized religion "aims to please."

The Biblical idea that "It is easier for a camel to pass through the eye of a needle than for a rich man to enter the kingdom of Heaven" has been edited for the '90s to: "The hump has shrunk." And the Bible has been translated, tranquilized, and sterilized so that there's a version for everybody. It's now appearing on the back of toilets, replacing other books of proverbs such as Don't Squat With Your Spurs On.

The Good Book includes parables that allow guys to soft pedal certain issues that are near and dear to them. Take drinking, where abstinence doesn't necessarily spawn piety. I've heard fresh inductees into the God Squad proclaim, "Jesus loved a good party! Look at his first miracle, water into wine!" Or "Dude, Noah was a drunk!"

Then there's sex, which the Bible-savvy guy will testify that God understood. Consider the fling Abraham had with Hagar the slave girl, which had to piss off his wife, Sarah, origins of the first menage a trois. Then there was David the shepherd boy, who went from king to home wrecker in Bathsheba's marriage to Uriah. And there was Samson, who fell under the spell of Delilah, who took delight in changing him from a ram to a lamb.

I believe men and women encounter God differently, and occasionally His heavenly directives can be mistaken for Satan's Hades Hotline. Take the epiphany I experienced once in a Neiman Marcus store.

The very fact that I was able to buy an original Bill Blass dress for 75 percent off was, well, it just doesn't happen. Those things NEVER go on sale! Right place at the right time? No. It was Divine Guidance. Period. But, my significant other at the time said it was "of the devil" when I couldn't pay the power bill the next month, which is why he became the insignificant one soon after.

Moral of the story? God is where we behold Him.

I certainly respect the poets in this chapter and their musings. But I think they may have assumed too much about the Almighty. After all, when God made man, She did it on Her lunch hour.

— kgs

THE QUEST

I sought Him on the purple seas,
I sought Him on the peaks aflame;
Amid the gloom of giant trees
And canyons lone I called His name;
The wasted ways of earth I trod:
In vain! In vain! I found not God.

I sought Him in the hives of men,
The cities grand, the hamlets grey,
The temples old beyond my ken,
The tabernacles of to-day;
All life that is, from cloud to clod I sought . . .
Alas! I found not God.

Then after roamings far and wide,
In streets and seas and deserts wild,
I came to stand at last beside
The death-bed of my little child.
Lo! as I bent beneath the rod
I raised my eyes . . . and there was God.

— Robert Service

THE YEAR'S AT THE SPRING

The year's at the spring,
And day's at the morn;
Morning's at seven;
The hillside's dew-pearled;
The lark's on the wing;
The snail's on the thorn:
God's in His Heaven—
All's right with the world!

— Robert Browning

THE LATEST DECALOGUE

Thou shalt have one God only; who
Would be at the expense of two?
No graven images may be
Worshipped, except the currency:
Swear not at all; for, for thy curse
Thine enemy is none the worse:
At church on Sunday to attend
Will serve to keep the world thy friend:
Honour thy parents; that is, all
From whom advancement may befall:
Thou shalt not kill; but need'st not strive
Officiously to keep alive:
Do not adultery commit;
Advantage rarely comes of it:
Thou shalt not steal; an empty feat,
When it's so lucrative to cheat:
Bear not false witness; let the lie
Have time on its own wings to fly:
Thou shalt not covet, but tradition
Approves all forms of competition.

— Arthur Hugh Clough

LIGHT SHINING OUT OF DARKNESS

God moves in a mysterious way,
    His wonders to perform;
He plants his footsteps in the sea,
    And rides upon the storm.

Deep in unfathomable mines
    Of never-failing skill,
He treasures up his bright designs,
    And works his sovereign will.

Ye fearful saints fresh courage take,
    The clouds ye so much dread
Are big with mercy, and shall break
    In blessings on your head.

Judge not the Lord by feeble sense,
    But trust him for his grace;
Behind a frowning providence,
    He hides a smiling face.

His purposes will ripen fast,
    Unfolding ev'ry hour;
The bud may have a bitter taste,
    But sweet will be the flow'r.

Blind unbelief is sure to err,
    And scan his work in vain;
God is his own interpreter,
    And he will make it plain.

— William Cowper

THE LORD IS MY SHEPHERD

The Lord is my shepherd; I shall not want.
He maketh me to lie down in green pastures: he leadeth me
beside the still waters.
He restoreth my soul: he leadeth me in the paths of righteousness
for his name's sake.
Yea, though I walk through the valley of the shadow of death, I
will fear no evil: for thou art with me; thy rod and thy staff
they comfort me.
Thou preparest a table before me in the presence of mine ene-
mies: thou anointest my head with oil; my cup runneth over.
Surely goodness and mercy shall follow me all the days of my life:
and I will dwell in the house of the Lord for ever.

— Psalm XXIII

"How They Feel"

A t last we reach the chapter on love, and you scoff. Ha! A woman's thing. Nay, nay my foolish friend. Hell may be equated with the fury of a woman scorned, but a jilted man is one of life's most tragic creatures. My God, how they can screw their lives up over a woman.

Women know their place. We're accustomed to the double standard and know innately that we're going to be lied to, cheated on, and traded in for a newer model with better performance on curves. The guys can still claim better gas mileage, however.

But men assume they're above it, that they aren't subject to the laws of love, one of them being: You only pass this way once, so love the one you're with or go.

Guys turn into automatons when their love has been spurned. They respond by getting drunk a lot followed by auditions for a quick, easy replacement, preferably someone who can cook.

That was one nice thing about early poets. They were strictly romantics who concentrated on beauty and didn't care about housework or food. And nobody from MCI ever called them during dinner.

Ah, love, that elusive buttercup amidst life's steel snares with teeth that hold us captive, causing some to gnaw their feet off rather than wait for the slow, inevitable death of a relationship.

And where does love go when it goes away? I see it as an amorphous haze that follows the jetstream and lands on the same planet with data blipped from computer screens, socks from the dryer, and people sucked out of airplanes.

Studies on Dan Cupid showed that for a fat, flying cherub he was a lousy shot with an arrow. He pierced many a heart, but sometimes the process broke them. Frankly, I find the little lard-butt a damn nuisance and wish he'd give up bow-hunting and put in for a rifle permit.

If you ask a guy if he agreed that "it was better to have loved and lost than never to have loved at all," most likely he'd answer, "Hell, no." But the poet would respond, "Ah, yes," for he knows that love never dies, it's merely born again.

In this chapter, Edgar Allan Poe leaves me weak as he writes of an enduring love in his poem, "Annabel Lee." And Shakespeare's sonnets, at least the ones included here, are so delicately intense, I think he must have run women off.

And as for Brautigan's "Love Poem," I would like to add that it goes both ways, buster!

— kgs

SHE WALKS IN BEAUTY

She walks in Beauty, like the night
    Of cloudless climes and starry skies;
And all that's best of dark and bright
    Meet in her aspect and her eyes:
Thus mellowed to that tender light
    Which Heaven to gaudy day denies.

One shade the more, one ray the less,
    Had half impaired the nameless grace
Which waves in every raven tress,
    Or softly lightens o'er her face;
Where thoughts serenely sweet express,
    How pure, how dear their dwelling-place.

And on that cheek, and o'er that brow,
    So soft, so calm, yet eloquent,
The smiles that win, the tints that glow,
    But tell of days in goodness spent,
A mind at peace with all below,
    A heart whose love is innocent!

— Lord Byron

A FAMILIAR PLACE

As we hunted frogs with BB guns,
my friend and I knew our place,
walking lightly behind tall ferns
before dark water like isinglass.

We had followed the bellow of a bullfrog
to its head, bigger than a lily pod,
beside a slanted, rotting snag.
But when we aimed, behind that wood

something moved. We craned our necks
and saw her face first under his,
then, against his hips her bobby socks
and next to her his boots, her shoes,

her shorts, his jeans all wadded up.
They moved and moved then motion locked;
she screamed then tensed her hips.
When I saw her tears, I slowly backed

up the bank, knocking loose a stone
that clattered down and splashed so loud
the frog ducked under, and the man,
uncoupled, slick and pink, stood

up and grabbed a real gun: blacker,
heavier than either of ours;
so we skidded and stumbled up the shore
while through budding trees, the early stars

sputtered too bright too soon
like the last look of hate on her face
as cold, white and still as the moon
yet as familiar as that place.
                                    — Greg Keeler

ANNABEL LEE

It was many and many a year ago,
        In a kingdom by the sea,
That a maiden there lived whom you may know
        By the name of Annabel Lee;
And this maiden she lived with no other thought
        Than to love and be loved by me.

She was a child and *I* was a child,
        In this kingdom by the sea,
But we loved with a love that was more than love—
        I and my Annabel Lee—
With a love that the winged seraphs of Heaven
        Coveted her and me.

And this was the reason that, long ago,
        In this kingdom by the sea,
A wind blew out of a cloud by night
        Chilling my Annabel Lee;
So that her high-born kinsmen came
        And bore her away from me,
To shut her up in a sepulchre
        In this kingdom by the sea.

The angels, not half so happy in Heaven,
　　Went envying her and me:—
Yes! that was the reason (as all men know,
　　In this kingdom by the sea)
That the wind came out of the cloud chilling
　　And killing my Annabel Lee.

But our love it was stronger by far than the love
　　Of those who were older than we—
　　Of many far wiser than we—
And neither the angels in Heaven above
　　Nor the demons down under the sea
Can ever dissever my soul from the soul
　　Of the beautiful Annabel Lee:—

For the moon never beams without bringing me dreams
　　Of the beautiful Annabel Lee:
And the stars never rise but I feel the bright eyes
　　Of the beautiful Annabel Lee:
And so all the night-tide, I lie down by the side
Of my darling, my darling, my life and my bride
　　In her sepulchre there by the sea—
　　In her tomb by the side of the sea.

— Edgar Allan Poe

I FEEL HORRIBLE. SHE DOESN'T

I feel horrible. She doesn't
love me and I wander around
the house like a sewing machine
that's just finished sewing
a turd to a garbage can lid.

— Richard Brautigan

"?"

If you had the choice of the two women to wed,
(Though of course the idea is quite absurd)
And the first from her heels to her dainty head
Was charming in every sense of the word:
And yet in the past (I grieve to state),
She never had been exactly "straight."

And the second—she was beyond all cavil,
A model of virtue, I must confess;
And yet, alas! she was dull as the devil,
And rather a dowd in the way of dress;
Though what she was lacking in wit and beauty,
She more than made up for in "sense of duty."

Now, suppose you must wed, and make no blunder
And either would love you, and let you win her—
Which of the two would you choose, I wonder,
The stolid saint or the sparkling sinner?

— Robert Service

LOVE POEM

It's so nice
to wake up in the morning
all alone
and not have to tell somebody
you love them
when you don't love them
anymore.

— Richard Brautigan

SHALL I COMPARE THEE TO A SUMMER'S DAY?

Shall I compare thee to a summer's day?
Thou art more lovely and more temperate:
Rough winds do shake the darling buds of May,
And summer's lease hath all too short a date;
Sometime too hot the eye of heaven shines,
And often is his gold complexion dimm'd;
And every fair from fair sometime declines,
By chance or nature's changing course untrimm'd:
But thy eternal summer shall not fade
Nor lose possession of that fair thou ow'st;
Nor shall Death brag thou wand'rest in his shade,
When in eternal lines to time thou grow'st;
    So long as men can breathe or eyes can see,
    So long lives this, and this gives life to thee.

— William Shakespeare

THE RETURN

They turned him loose; he bowed his head,
    A felon, bent and grey.
His face was even as the Dead,
    He had no word to say.

He sought the home of his old love,
    To look on her once more;
And where her roses breathed above,
    He cowered beside the door.

She sat there in the shining room;
    Her hair was silver grey.
He stared and stared from out the gloom;
    He turned to go away.

Her roses rustled overhead.
    She saw, with sudden start.
"I knew that you would come," she said,
    And held him to her heart.

Her face was rapt and angel-sweet;
    She touched his hair of grey;
But he, sob-shaken, at her feet,
    Could only pray and pray.

— Robert Service

WHEN, IN DISGRACE WITH FORTUNE AND MEN'S EYES

When, in disgrace with fortune and men's eyes,
I all alone beweep my outcast state,
And trouble deaf heaven with my bootless cries,
And look upon myself, and curse my fate,
Wishing me like to one more rich in hope,
Featured like him, like him with friends possessed,
Desiring this man's art, and that man's scope,
With what I most enjoy contented least;
Yet in these thoughts myself almost despising,
Haply I think on thee, and then my state,
Like to the lark at break of day arising
From sullen earth, sings hymns at heaven's gate;
    For thy sweet love remembered such wealth brings
    That then I scorn to change my state with kings.

— William Shakespeare

HYMN TO DOGS

You walk sideways and forward
all at once panting.
How can we hold the torn trash
and night barking against you?
We should kill you,
freeze-dry your meat
and send you salted
to our starving,
but instead
we pave your way
with scraps from our tables
and take you on walks
where your bodily functions
excuse our lack of direction.
Given the chance,
you'll bathe in carrion
or lap your puke
then return radiant
to kiss us on our mouths.
Blind, we follow you.
Deaf, we watch you listen.
Dumb, we empathize.
You teach our young
the pain of love,
knotted together
backwards and yelping.
We've sent you spinning
from the bumpers of our cars
and had to stop and polish you off
in full light of your bleeding grin.

— Greg Keeler

THOSE WINTER SUNDAYS

Sundays too my father got up early
and put his clothes on in the blueblack cold,
then with cracked hands that ached
from labor in the weekday weather made
banked fires blaze. No one ever thanked him.

I'd wake and hear the cold splintering, breaking.
When the rooms were warm, he'd call,
and slowly I would rise and dress,
fearing the chronic angers of that house,

Speaking indifferently to him,
who had driven out the cold
and polished my good shoes as well.
What did I know, what did I know
of love's austere and lonely offices?

— Robert Hayden

THIS IS JUST TO SAY

I have eaten
the plums
that were in
the icebox

and which
you were probably
saving
for breakfast

Forgive me
they were delicious
so sweet
and so cold.

— William Carlos Williams

FAREWELL! THOU ART TOO DEAR FOR MY POSSESSING

Farewell! thou art too dear for my possessing,
 And like enough thou know'st thy estimate:
The charter of thy worth gives thee releasing;
 My bonds in thee are all determinate.
For how do I hold thee but by thy granting?
 And for that riches where is my deserving?
The cause of this fair gift in me is wanting,
 And so my patent back again is swerving.
Thyself thou gav'st, thy own worth then not knowing,
 Or me, to whom thou gav'st it, else mistaking;
So thy great gift, upon misprision growing,
 Comes home again, on better judgment making.
  Thus have I had thee, as a dream doth flatter,
  In sleep a king, but, waking, no such matter.

— William Shakespeare

WEDDING

I with my new job
and you with your son, Chris,
decide that matrimony
is a must, so we kiss
sin and the 60's goodbye and head
for Elko, Nevada and a no questions,
no blood test, quick-fix solution.
The casinos, whore-house trailers,
Basque food joints and shopping malls
all say THIS IS THE PLACE
TO MAKE SACRED OUR LOVE,
and after we find the grand court house
the Justice of the Peace does,
as blue-haired court clerks
weep and clasp their hands
and Chris stares dumb
at his mom and new dad.
With no wedding rings,
we use those from your ears
then follow the Justice
to a private room where
he tells us some jokes
and of duck hunting in Cuba
before it fell—when everyone drove
Continentals and 300 ducks
could be shot in one day.
We say how much do we owe.
He says whatever it's worth.
So from a fat roll of twenties
you pull out a five and we go.

— Greg Keeler

THE BETROTHED

"You must choose between me and your cigar"
Open the old cigar-box, get me a Cuba stout,
For things are running crossways, and Maggie and I are out.

We quarreled about Havanas—we fought o'er a good cheroot,
And I know she is exacting, and she says I am a brute.

Open the old cigar-box—let me consider a space;
In the soft blue veil of the vapor, musing on Maggie's face.

Maggie is pretty to look at—Maggie's a loving lass,
But the prettiest cheeks must wrinkle, the truest of loves
    must pass.

There's peace in a Laranaga, there's calm in a Henry Clay,
But the best cigar in an hour is finished and thrown away—

Thrown away for another as perfect and ripe and brown—
But I could not throw away Maggie for fear o' the talk
    o' the town!

Maggie, my wife at fifty—gray and dour and old—
With never another Maggie to purchase for love or gold!

And the light of Days that have Been, the dark of the Days
    that Are,
And Love's torch stinking stale, like the butt of a dead cigar—

The butt of a dead cigar you are bound to keep in your pocket—
With never a new one to light tho' it's charred and black to
    the socket.

Open the old cigar-box—let me consider a while—
Here is a mild Manilla—there is a wifely smile.

Which is the better portion—bondage bought with a ring,
Or a harem of dusky beauties, fifty tied in a string?

Counselors cunning and silent—comforters true and tried,
And never a one of the fifty to sneer at a rival bride.

Thought in the early morning, solace in time of woes,
Peace in the hush of the twilight, balm ere my eyelids close.

This will the fifty give me, asking naught in return,
With only a Suttee's passion—to do their duty and burn.

This will the fifty give me, when they are spent and dead,
Five times other fifties shall be my servants instead.

The furrows of far-off Java, the isles of the Spanish Main,
When they hear my harem is empty, will send me my brides
    again.

I will take no heed to their raiment, nor food for their mouths
    withal,
So long as the gulls are nesting, so long as the showers fall.

I will scent 'em with best vanilla, with tea will I temper their
    hides,
And the Moor and the Mormon shall envy who read of the tale
    of my brides.

For Maggie has written a letter to give me my choice between
The wee little whimpering Love and the great god Nick o' Teen.

And I have been servant of Love for barely a twelvemonth clear,
But I have been Priest of Partagas a matter of seven year;

And the gloom of my bachelor days is flecked with the cheery
    light
Of stumps that I burned to Friendship and Pleasure and Work
    and Fight.

And I turn my eyes to the future that Maggie and I must prove,
But the only light on the marshes is the Will-o'-the-Wisp of
    Love.

Will it see me safe through my journey, or leave me bogged in
    the mire?
Since a puff of tobacco can cloud it, shall I follow the fitful fire?

Open the old cigar-box—let me consider anew—
Old friends, and who is Maggie that I should abandon you?

A million surplus Maggies are willing to bear the yoke;
And a woman is only a woman, but a good cigar is a Smoke.

Light me another Cuba; I hold to my first-sworn vows
If Maggie will have no rival, I'll have no Maggie for spouse!

—Rudyard Kipling

CHAPTER 10

"Whatever"

⊱┈┈♦┈─O─┈♦┈┈⊰

W ell, here we are at the final chapter, and its poems are perhaps the most thought-provoking. They elicit a certain wistfulness while recalling passages in life, and the people, places, and things that we leave behind for whatever reason.

Service and Keeler remind us that home is where the heart is, whether it's a cabin in the woods, a double-wide trailer with tires on top, or a goldfish bowl. It seems to be not so much what it is, but what it stands for.

I know how men value their getaway retreats. One of my former husbands allowed me to visit his "sanctuary" once. And while congratulating myself on being invited to the inner sanctum, I slithered beneath the bed linens, which had not been freshened since dinosaurs roamed the earth. Ignoring the grimy sheets, I awaited my host, who was preparing mood-enhancing beverages. Suddenly I felt footsteps of the furry sort plodding up my back and before I could react, the stinging began. Screaming and writhing, I became wrapped cocoon-like in the sour sheets and learned that hornets were the landlords.

And did my darling dipwad assist me? No, his ego translated the scene to mean that I was out of control in anticipation of sharing cocktails with him in bed. So it was definitely good-bye little cabin. Give me the Ritz.

But Service made me proud to be a woman when I read his poem about the angel that visited earth. At last, a sort of role reversal where a guy angel fell victim to the wiles of a predatory, secular woman, forcing his Master to get the hook.

And, oh, that I could find the thrill in a Swiss Army knife that Keeler does. That's so cute, so guy-like. What other species could sit for hours and play with an instrument the size of their finger, something that sticks, pokes, screws, picks, and pulls? A gizmo that thrives on splinters and errant body hair.

That's why poetry is so wonderful. An escape, a flight of fancy where the mundane is transcended and little things come alive with meaning. Isn't it sad that the only "little things" some men know are the tips they give a valet parking boy?

You may be surprised, as I was, that poet Burgess had never seen a purple cow. Not only have I seen a bossy of lavender hue, after a few drinks I married one, too.

And finally, Keeler's piece, "Vasectomy," besides making me wonder if it was performed with a Swiss Army knife, is a puzzling verse on which the editor guy chose to end the book.

After all, what did *Poetry for Guys* begin with? Sports. Which takes us back to my original supposition. Main things a guy thinks about? Sports and sex. You'll never convince me otherwise.

And congratulations, boys. You've almost completed a course on becoming a sensitive '90s guy. But know what? We liked you anyway.

— kgs

GOOD-BYE, LITTLE CABIN

O dear little cabin, I've loved you so long,
And now I must bid you good-bye!
I've filled you with laughter, I've thrilled you with song
And sometimes I've wished I could cry.
Your walls they have witnessed a weariful fight,
And rung to a won Waterloo:
But oh, in my triumph I'm dreary to-night—
Good-bye, little cabin, to you!

Your roof is bewhiskered, your floor is a-slant,
Your walls seem to sag and to swing;
I'm trying to find-just your faults, but I can't—
You poor, tired, heart-broken old thing!
I've seen when you've been the best friend that I had
Your light like a gem on the snow;
You're sort of a part of me—Gee! but I'm sad;
I hate, little cabin, to go.

Below your cracked window red raspberries climb;
A hornet's nest hangs from a beam;
Your rafters are scribbled with adage and rhyme,
And dimmed with tobacco and dream.
"Each day has its laugh," and "Don't worry, just work."
Such mottoes reproachfully shine.
Old calendars dangle—what memories lurk
About you, dear cabin of mine!

I hear the world-call and the clang of the fight;
I hear the hoarse cry of my kind;
Yet well do I know, as I quit you to-night,
It's Youth that I'm leaving behind
And often I'll think of you, empty and black,

Moose antlers nailed over your door
Oh, if I should perish my ghost will come back
To dwell in you, cabin, once more!

How cold, still and lonely, how weary you seem!
A last wistful look and I'll go
Oh, will you remember the lad with his dream!
The lad that you comforted so
The shadows enfold you, it's drawing to-night;
The evening star needles the sky
And huh! but it's stinging and stabbing my sight—
God bless you, old cabin, good-bye!

— Robert Service

AQUARIUM

In their little box of water they drift by
beside the window in my living room.
They pause between the glass walls and then resume
their sullen orbit till the day they die.
Sometimes one, with slightly tilted eye,
seems perhaps to realize its doom
but more likely to judge the vapid goon
who's staring in. That tilt just might imply—
"Poor Greg, I pity you out there
in your little box of air, wearing a path
to match your bodily functions: a waking nightmare
from living room to kitchen to bed room to bath
room. I thank God that in here I can go where I wish
to live, eat, breed, sleep and poop—one free fish."

— Greg Keeler

136

SWISS ARMY SERMON

Blessed is thy little saw,
for it shall secure us
blunt and tidy weenie sticks.
Blessed is thy combination bottle-opener
screwdriver, for with it,
we shall pry many nails.
Blessed is thy plastic toothpick,
for our children shall use it
to pop Bowser's ticks.
Blessed are thy little scissors,
for we shall be at their mercy
while trimming our nose-hairs
on bumpy backroads in pickups.
Blessed is thy can opener
which we shall never learn to use
even though Uncle Walt
makes it look so simple and says,
"Jesus, I thought I showed you
how to use this damn thing last summer."
Blessed are thy tweezers,
for with them we shall obliterate
the skin around our splinter
so that we shall never find it.
Blessed is thy big blade,
for with it our children will learn
why Uncle Walt told them to never
carve toward themselves.
Blessed is thy little blade,
for with it we shall eventually
be able to remove the stitches.
Blessed is thy reamer

which folds obscurely into thy back,
for it shall be kept from closing
entirely by thy key ring thus
punching us in our privates when we
return thee to our pocket.
Blessed is thy key ring,
for thy large bulk will keep us from
losing our tiny key until we leave thee
sticking in the river bank,
tiny key and all.
Blessed is thy corkscrew,
for it shall shred our corks
until we have to push them down
into our wine with a stick.

— Greg Keeler

THE PURPLE COW

I never saw a Purple Cow,
    I never hope to see one;
But I can tell you, anyhow,
    I'd rather see than be one.

— Gelett Burgess

THE WOMAN AND THE ANGEL

An angel was tired of heaven, as he lounged in the golden
    street;
His halo was tilted sideways, and his harp lay mute at his feet;
So the Master stooped in His pity, and gave him a pass to go,
For the space of a moon, to the earth-world, to mix with the
    men below.

He doffed his celestial garments, scarce waiting to lay them
    straight;
He bade good-by to Peter, who stood by the golden gate;
The sexless singers of heaven chanted a fond farewell,
And the imps looked up as they pattered on the red-hot flags of
    hell.

Never was seen such an angel—eyes of heavenly blue,
Features that shamed Apollo, hair of a golden hue;
The women simply adored him; his lips were like Cupid's bow;
But he never ventured to use them—and so they voted him
    slow.

Till at last there came One Woman, a marvel of loveliness,
And she whispered to him: "Do you love me?" And he
    answered that woman, "Yes."
And she said: "Put your arms around me, and kiss me, and
    hold me—so—"
But fiercely he drew back, saying: "This thing is wrong, and I
    know."

Then sweetly she mocked his scruples, and softly she him
    beguiled:
"You, who are verily man among men, speak with the tongue of
    a child.

We have outlived the old standards; we have burst, like an over-
    tight thong,
The ancient, outworn, Puritanic traditions of Right and Wrong."

Then the Master feared for His angel, and called him again to
    His side,
For oh, the woman was wondrous, and oh, the angel was tried!
And deep in his hell sang the Devil, and this was the strain of
    his song:
"The ancient, outworn, Puritanic traditions of Right and
    Wrong."

— Robert Service

ANYONE LIVED IN A PRETTY HOW TOWN

anyone lived in a pretty how town
(with up so floating many bells down)
spring summer autumn winter
he sang his didn't he danced his did.

Women and men (both little and small)
cared for anyone not at all
they sowed their isn't they reaped their same
sun moon stars rain

children guessed (but only a few
and down they forgot as up they grew
autumn winter spring summer)
that noone loved him more by more

when by now and tree by leaf
she laughed his joy she cried his grief
bird by snow and stir by still
anyone's any was all to her

someones married their everyones
laughed their cryings and did their dance
(sleep wake hope and then) they said
their nevers they slept their dream

stars rain sun moon
(and only the snow can begin to explain
how children are apt to forget to remember
with up so floating many bells down)

one day anyone died i guess
(and noone stooped to kiss his face)
busy folk buried them side by side
little by little and was by was

all by all and deep by deep
and more by more they dream their sleep
noone and anyone earth by april
wish by spirit and if by yes.

Women and men (both dong and ding)
summer autumn winter spring
reaped their sowing and went their came
sun moon stars rain

— e.e. cummings

THE JOY OF LITTLE THINGS

It's good the great green earth to roam,
Where sights of awe the soul inspire;
But oh, it's best, the coming home,
The crackle of one's own hearth-fire!
You've hob-nobbed with the solemn Past;
You've seen the pageantry of kings;
Yet oh, how sweet to gain at last
The peace and rest of Little Things!

Perhaps you're counted with the Great;
You strain and strive with mighty men;
Your hand is on the helm of State;
Colossus-like you stride . . . and then
There comes a pause, a shining hour,
A dog that leaps, a hand that clings:
O Titan, turn from pomp and power;
Give all your heart to Little Things.

Go couch you childwise in the grass,
Believing it's some jungle strange,
Where mighty monsters peer and pass,
Where beetles roam and spiders range.
'Mid gloom and gleam of leaf and blade,
What dragons rasp their painted wings!
O magic world of shine and shade!
O beauty land of Little Things!

I sometimes wonder, after all,
Amid this tangled web of fate,
If what is great may not be small,
And what is small may not be great.

"WHATEVER"

So wondering I go my way,
Yet in my heart contentment sings . . .
O may I ever see, I pray,
God's grace and love in Little Things.

So give to me, I only beg,
A little roof to call my own,
A little cider in the keg,
A little meat upon the bone;
A little garden by the sea,
A little boat that dips and swings . . .
Take wealth, take fame, but leave to me,
O Lord of Life, just Little Things.

— Robert Service

VASECTOMY

waiting for an hour alone
in the white room

naked from the waist down
clean flesh on clean sheets

polished steel and rubber tubes
behind reminiscences

of alcibiades on his*
lopping spree (would bogart

do this) and the doctor
in his cowboy boots

(did you hear the one
about the steer)

when wife had first child
she stood outside herself

listened to a distant scream
but this is different

even in the local numbness
my feet and neck converge

with the lifting of the cords
then fall back with the cutting

exhausted and sweating
I view my progeny

two segments like macaroni
stuck to the steel tray

— Greg Keeler

* Alcibiades: A Greek who ran around knocking the penises off of statues.